How to Polis

Joe Dawson

www.joedauthor.com

@joedauthor1

ISBN 978-0-9956904-0-0

Dead Leg Publishing

How to Polish a Turd

By Billy Travis

About the Author

Billy Travis wrote his first novel, *How to Polish a Turd*, on the back of a toilet roll while trapped in a portaloo at Brownload Fest. Billy's hobbies include brushing his teeth, doing a wee, and putting his clothes in the washing machine when they are dirty and need a wash.

To You

To the reader,

This book has thoroughly been edited by experts from NASA. Any mistakes found are the responsibility of the reader, not the author. Nevertheless, please send any grammatical complaints to NASA. The author is an innocent man.

Foreword (and Forewarning)

I volunteered to write this foreword, for I feel it is my duty to save society. I am baffled why anybody would purchase this book. It is inconceivable that anybody throughout Earth's entire history could get any pleasure out of reading this dribble that you may call a book, but what I call the aborted infant of Dracula and Frankenstein. There is no reason why this insufferable nonsense exists, nor does it have a purpose, except maybe to be used as a bum wad if you are stuck on the john and want to save toilet paper (a blank roll of toilet paper would be a better read than this dribble).

The arrogance of the author is shocking. Billy Travis has the cheek to try to disguise this vacuous book as an intelligent book disguised as a vacuous book. There is a place reserved in the sixth circle of Hell for this hypocrite. There are so many contradictions within his prose that he himself must be seen as a walking paradox. His lack of description further shows his incapability to string a sentence together, while the little research he has done probably came from Wikipedia.

There are only seven good books in the world; this is not one of them. If this book somehow becomes popular, which is inevitable because Stephen Hawking and I are the only two intelligent people left on this planet of dimwits, not only will it be pernicious to the book industry, but it will signify the death of art. When that day comes, I pray for Beatrice to guide me to the high heavens, so I may ask God why he stole Shakespeare's ideas to create Earth.

Smug Regards,

The Blooming Harold

Contents

One

Screw Jacob Marley; the only spirit Burger Barry worried about was the ghost of Colonel Sanders shoving a chicken drummer up his arse.

'Rodney! I'm not paying you to slack off, darn it!' Rodney's lunchtime wasn't over, yet Barry's outburst was expected. Scrooge of the burger industry acted like a midget who's been put in a dishwasher for a reason: world domination was a push away. Burger Hole's competition was almost dead. Burger King alienated most of their customers when the King gave control of the burger monarchy to North Korea. Burger Korea was exactly the same as Burger King, except you weren't allowed inside the restaurant.

'My lunch isn't over for another five minutes.'

'Darn it, Rodney, the World Health inspector is here today. I'm up to here with stress without your attitude. There's a line of hungry customers out there. You will give them their daily dose of burgers, or else.'

Rodney groaned and put his Burger Hole hat on. Burger Barry hadn't lied; he desperately wanted to give the public their daily dose of burgers. His mission statement was to give as many people gout as he could.

Rodney stepped onto the empty restaurant floor. *Line of hungry customers, eh?*

Beside him, the World Health inspector called Barry over. 'Well,' the inspector said. 'I have found that over seventy-five percent of your food contains shrapnel from the Vietnam War. Your fish fillets contain a variation of the black death that hasn't been active since 1353, and I found a dead cat in your Coke supply. All in all, I'd say those are some fine natural ingredients. Five stars.'

Barry wiped the sweat from his forehead. There was no need for him to get so heated; it wouldn't have mattered if the inspector had have given them one star. Customers were happy to eat a turd smothered in breadcrumbs as long as it was served to them in under two minutes. It wouldn't make any difference if Barry warned the public about the risks of eating his food. 'Eat that double-cheese cheeseburger, sir, but I'm warning you now—your cock will fall off.'

'Depends, do I get a large Coke and fries for my troubles?'

'Yes.'

'Ah go on then, it'll be worth it.'

Rodney shook his head and put his elbows on the counter. 'Whoa, slick,' said Tom Wat, a man whose signature described him perfectly. 'If a customer came up to buy something, what would they think?'

'They're happy to buy food from a restaurant accused of making their burgers out of duck arseholes. I doubt they'd care.'

Tom tutted. 'You just make sure you have a smile on your face when a customer comes in.'

Rodney sighed and put his elbows back on the counter. A bubbly woman entered the restaurant—a woman so bubbly that if an officer came around in the middle of the night to tell her that her husband was dead, she would probably burst out laughing. 'It's beautiful weather today,' she said, wearing a big grin.

'Yup.'

'I bet you're unhappy you're stuck indoors all day.' Her ginormous grin took over her entire face.

'You gonna order summat, then?' Rodney heard Tom cough behind him. He refused to turn around.

The bubbly woman rubbed her chin. 'Let me think…I think I'll have…Yes, I'll have a pepperoni slice, please.'

Rodney groaned. 'This is Burger Hole, love.'

'So?'

'We don't sell pepperoni slices. We sell burgers, albeit burnt ones made of duck arseholes.'

'Ahem,' came from behind Rodney.

Rodney turned around. 'What?'

'What are you are doing?' Tom whispered in Rodney's ear.

'I'm trying to sell a burger, if you don't mind.'

'That is not how to treat a customer.'

'Why?'

'Because of the way you said *we don't sell pepperoni slices.*'

'What?' Rodney all but shouted. 'We don't sell pepperoni slices. What do you expect me to do? Give her a cheeseburger and hope she doesn't notice the difference?'

DYK? You can tell how old someone is by asking them how old they are.

This is page **2.**

'Look. Let me handle this before she storms out the shop.'

'I don't think we're in danger of that happening.' Rodney looked at the bubbly woman. She looked like she was suppressing a giggle as she stared at the bubbling fat fryer. Rodney couldn't believe by the expression of wonder on her face that they were in Burger Hole.

Tom turned toward the bubbly woman. 'HIYA, LOVE,' he said, loud and slowly. 'I'M SORRY TO SAY WE DON'T HAVE ANY PEPPERONI SLICES, I'M AFRAID.' Rodney half-expected Tom to lean over the counter to pat the woman on the head. 'WOULD YOU BE INTERESTED IN BUYING A BURGER INSTEAD? IF YOU LOOK ABOVE YOUR HEAD, YOU WILL SEE WE HAVE A MENU.'

The woman gasped. 'Ooh, a menu. How modern.' Rodney began to wonder whether this woman had ever stepped out of her house before.

Tom gave the woman his best toothy smile. 'IT'S ALMOST A BAD THING,' he joked. 'CUSTOMERS STAND HERE ALL DAY BECAUSE THEY'RE SPOILT FOR CHOICE,' he said, adding a laugh on the end.

The woman laughed as if Tom had just pulled a horse out of his arse. 'It's a crazy world we live in now,' she said, wiping a tear from her eye. 'Back in my day, we had nothing to eat but rations of spam.'

'You say "back in your day" as if you used to own a slot in the week,' Rodney moaned.

'OOH NO,' Tom interrupted. 'I COULDN'T POSSIBLY LIVE OFF SPAM. I'D MISS MY WET LETTUCE TOO MUCH, HA-HA. BUT YOU KNOW WHAT THEY SAY. FIVE BURGERS A DAY KEEPS THE DOCTOR AWAY.' Tom held up five fingers, in case the woman had somehow not understood his loud talking.

'Gosh,' the woman laughed. 'I better get my fill before the sun sets. I'll have five guacamole burgers, love.'

Tom struggled to get the price up on the register, and the woman made some crack about how that meant the food was free. Eventually, the price came up, and never before had Rodney seen someone so happy to pay twenty-five pounds for five dry slabs of meat covered in green stuff that looked and smelt like it had come straight from a sewer in Mexico. Tom was as happy as the woman. 'You see. You've got to make a connection with the customer. You've got to make them feel warm and loved.'

'Oh, aye. Everyone comes to Burger Hole to be loved. There's nothing more romantic than eating a guacamole burger.'

Tom ignored Rodney as he watched a woman in a fur coat approach the counter. 'Why don't you serve this woman, Rodney? If you find yourself struggling, think of what I'd do.'

'I've worked here longer than you, Tom—' Rodney cut himself off when he noticed Tom had left the restaurant floor. *Great*. He was free to put his elbows back on the counter. The fur-coat woman marched up to the counter, folded her arms, and huffed. Rodney stared, waiting for her to say something. Like all good customer-service workers, he broke the awkward silence. '*Wot?*'

The woman snorted. 'I've been looking around this establishment for ten minutes, yet I cannot find a knife and fork anywhere.' Appropriately, she sounded like a woman who used a knife and fork to pick her nose.

'This is Burger Hole, love. We don't do cutlery.' She was lucky to have a table, considering the location of the restaurant. Most people in Bradford ate their dinner off the floor.

The woman stomped her feet. 'How am I supposed to eat my food without a knife and fork?'

'Use your hands.'

'And get food on my wedding ring?'

'Argh, you'll get sick of seeing it eventually anyway.'

'What kind of grubby eating establishment is this?' the woman yelled. 'I heard this was a sophisticated restaurant!'

'Do you live under a rock? This is Burger Hole, love. If you don't mind me asking, have you been hit over the head recently?'

Barry stormed out of the back. 'What's the darn problem here?'

The woman spoke before Rodney could open his mouth. 'This man is useless and rude. I asked for a knife and fork, and he told me to eat with my hands.'

'He did, did he?' Sweat dripped down Barry's face.

'I must say, I am very disappointed with my experience here. I booked a day off work to come here, yet I can't even eat my food.'

Rodney shook his head. *Who books work off to eat at Burger Hole?*

'What if he fed you?' Barry suggested. 'What if he used his hands to place the food in your mouth?'

Rodney's eyes widened; the woman rolled hers. 'I suppose that will have to do. I'll be waiting at my table.'

Rodney didn't care that the woman was still in earshot when he began to moan. 'Why the hell did you suggest that?'

'Somebody had to suggest it, darn it. You're throwing money away with your terrible service.'

'Can't you just give her a pair of gloves or something?'

'The customer has spoken, darn it, and by God, the customer is always right.'

Rodney held great disdain for the saying 'the customer is always right'; it encouraged people to act like nob heads.

'You get out there, Rodney, and you put your fingers in her mouth. You put your whole darn fist down her throat if she asks you to. Otherwise, I'll send you back to the jobcentre with the rest of Bradford.'

Reluctantly, Rodney fed the woman. Like the obedient customer-service worker he was, he went beyond what was required of him and put his hands in her mouth, risking infection and dexterity as she bit his fingers to bloody, bruised pulps before she told Barry that the service she received had been terrible. It didn't matter that Rodney had bled to please the customer; Barry still gave him a bollocking.

Four o'clock. *Finally.* Rodney got changed out of his Burger Hole clothes. He was about to walk out the door, when Tom called, 'See you tonight, slick.'

Rodney grunted. 'What the hell are you talking about?'

'The graveyard shift. Ben said he'd spoken to you; he told me you could cover his shift.' Ben hadn't spoken to Rodney, though that shouldn't have been a surprise. Ben was intolerable in the most harmless kind of way. He was the type of man who'd break into your house, steal nothing, only to do something really inconvenient like mixing up all your socks, or like leaving a massive dump on your bed.

Rodney grumbled. 'This is the first I've heard about it.'

'Really? Oh…Well, we've put your name down now, so you might as well work.'

Life tip: You should inhale and exhale air through your nose or mouth. This is called breathing. **5.**

'Can't you just rub my name off?'

'I don't know about that. It's written in marker pen. It'd make the rota look messy if we tried to rub it off.'

Rodney threw his arms up in the air. 'Pissing hell. I guess I'll see you tonight, then.'

'BYE-BYE!'

Rodney drove home in his crappy car and hated every song that came on the radio, despite the fact nobody was forcing him to listen to it. Someone overtook him just before he hit a queue, obviously desperate to get stuck in traffic before him. The reason for traffic was always the same; there was a bunch of men employed to make holes in the road.

Rodney was a good driver. He checked his phone while driving. *Ey up, nob head. Fancy coming to mine to watch the football?*

Rodney shuddered. It was bad enough he supported England—watching them around Johnny was even worse. Johnny became the angriest man alive when watching football. He couldn't go ten seconds without yelling at the tele. It was a cardinal sin to pass the ball backward, but God almighty forbid the referee to give a decision against England no matter how blatant the foul. England player throws a grenade at Brazil striker, receives a red card. 'Fuck off ref ya cheating bastard! He got the bloody ball!' Brazil striker taken off the pitch in a body bag. 'Get up ya soft bastard! Nowt wrong with ya!'

The games themselves didn't exactly excite Rodney. Hard to get excited for a match when the most entertaining thing was watching the England players pretend to sing 'God Save the Queen.'

Apart from getting angry at England, Johnny was all right—except he didn't know what banter was. Pulling someone's pants down? *Banter!* Lying naked in the Sahara Desert without any sun cream on? *Banter!* Doing a poo in a public toilet with the door unlocked? *Banter!* Johnny would get arrested for stabbing someone in the chest. 'Defendant, how do you plead?'

'Your Honour, it was just banter.'

'Oh, that's okay, then. We'll let you off.'

No, I do not want to watch football anywhere near you, Rodney thought. *Yes, pal. What time should I come up?* Rodney texted back.

Rodney's flat sat on a street where the kids unwrapped used

cigarettes for fun. He butted his head against the steering wheel when he recognised a car parked outside that belonged to one of Bridget's best mates. After a not-so-hard day at work, the last thing Rodney wanted to do was listen to Bridget's friends and their annoying boyfriends set the world to rights. If Bridget and her friends lived by the saying 'if you've got nothing good to say about someone, don't say anything at all,' they would never talk about anybody. Luckily, they didn't live by this saying, because all they did was talk about other people.

Rodney entered his flat to *Birmingham Ballbags* blaring on the tele. Jimmy Brummy was distraught he didn't win worst haircut of the decade, so his girlfriend decided to get a pair of boobs surgically added to her forehead to try and cheer him up. The latest slang coined by the show was the word 'exy'—in other words, still sexy without your ex. If Bridget continued to use the word 'exy' unsarcastically in real life, she might soon be able to use the word to describe herself—the 'ex' part, that is. I don't have to tell you how she looked. She was with Rodney after all, a man who at times looked like a deflated turd.

The tele was actually just background noise for the important chatter going on. Bridget, Alice and Oliver were so engrossed in conversation that they didn't notice Rodney come in.

'I thought ALDI couldn't get any worse after Mrs Fat-Arse left, but I was wrong.' Bridget said. If there was one thing she and Rodney had in common, it was that they hated work. 'You won't believe what's happened now.'

Alice's jaw dropped. 'Go on. Tell us.'

'A bloody twenty-year-old has been appointed manager.'

A shocked gasp that suggested the end of the world was nigh filled the air. 'No? You can't be serious?'

'Too bloody right I am. She looks like she stills goes to school, never mind overseeing the country's best supermarket.'

Alice shook her head in disgust. 'How could HR let this happen? Everybody knows that every single person under the age of twenty-five is an idiot.'

'Aye, well, you'll love this. You know what she did today. She asked me to go clean up the mess in aisle five. The bloody cheek.'

What does she think I'm there to do? Work? How dare she order me to do tasks I am contractually obliged to do.'

Alice and Oliver nodded in agreement. 'Clearly the power given to this girl has gone to her head,' Oliver concluded. Alice's boyfriend loved to give his 'expert' opinion on things. 'My guess is she had parents older than herself. That's why she feels the need to degrade people above her age.'

'That makes sense!' Alice cried. 'I bet she *did* have parents older than herself. That explains everything!'

Rodney noticed the can in Oliver's hand. 'You're drinking my beer.'

The light in Bridget's eyes died when she saw Rodney. She grabbed him by the arm and led him to the kitchen. Rodney overheard the 'psychologist' say, 'threatening people for sharing his girlfriend's drinks. I told you he was an alcoholic.'

It's my bloody beer, Rodney thought, but the 'psychologist' was probably right about him being an alcoholic, despite being wrong in his explanation to coming to the conclusion. Either way, it didn't lower Rodney's disdain for the man. A small part of Rodney wanted Bridget to have an affair with Oliver, just so he would have an excuse to punch him in the face. Really, Rodney was just jealous that Oliver had a girlfriend who actually liked him.

By the look on Bridget's face, they were well past the honeymoon phase. Her relationship expectations had been based on Disney films. She dreamt of a romantic man who would woo her every day. Imagine her disappointment the first time she came home and found Rodney sat on the sofa, playing on the Xbox in his jizz-stained underpants. Any hint of romance that may have lived inside him was blatantly dead. He was a man who didn't pay anything for his girlfriend's Christmas present anymore; he just gave her whatever he was given at work for Secret Santa. Regarding her love for Disney, she may or may not have been pleased that she looked like if Mowgli had smoked forty cigarettes a day for the last fifteen years.

Bridget's stare was enough to say her words. She spoke anyway. 'What are you doing here?'

'Sorry. Excuse me for entering the building I pay the rent for. I'll be on my way now. Really? Why else would I be here?'

'I *told you* I was having Alice and Oliver around for Eurovision.'

'You've invited your friends over to watch Eurovision?'

'Yes! We actually have a good act this time. We might win.' Hardly bloody likely. Put the politics to bed for one night they say, yet Sweden could send out a goat in a tutu, and Denmark would still give them twelve points. 'I want you out of the house, Rodney. I don't want you sitting around here being awkward.'

Rodney overheard Oliver say, 'can't even let his girlfriend have friends around. I told you he was a control freak.' Rodney couldn't take another remark from Oliver and left to get some fresh air.

He walked over a bridge overlooking a carpark. He had an epiphany. Did he really want to watch football with Johnny? Did he really want to spend the rest of his life with Bridget? Did he really want to spend another day selling cheeseburgers?

As he stood on the ledge of the bridge, an excited traffic warden walked by. He rubbed his hands together. 'Going to off yourself, are you?'

Rodney gave him a cockeyed look. 'Why are you so happy about it?'

'Your splattered body is going to make the police block off half the carpark. You don't know the joy I'm going to get from ticketing people for parking out on the road.'

'Well, I'd wish you the best in life, but I kind of wish people like you would join me.'

'No thanks. I'd hate my final moment to be by a parking meter. That's what I don't get about you suicidal folk. You pick the most boring places to die.'

'I'm about to die. Why do I care?'

'I'm just saying, why d'ya want the last thing you ever do to be to jump off a grubby structure into some sleazy carpark? Your money won't follow you to the grave—why not blow it all on a trip to the Antarctic? Feel freedom and run around naked with the penguins.' And with that utter abortion of a comment, Rodney decided to jump. The traffic warden shook his head. He'd be sure to place a parking ticket on Rodney's grave for revenge.

Bridget would receive a letter: Your boyfriend is buried under double yellow lines. Pay fifty quid, or we'll bring him back alive.

Wow-wa-woo-wah! What a cliffhanger! OMFG! Such good storytelling. I wonder if he really is dead? I've only read a chapter, yet the MAIN CHARACTER MAY ALREADY BE DEAD!

That's right! We'll be right back after this preview.

The Jimmy Daniels Show

Calling all late breakfast eaters—your favourite lunchtime show is back! No, not worn-out crap that's clogged up in the loft that we're still gonna get prissy over when we find out it's only worth a fiver, no! It's the Jimmy Daniels Show!

With everyday affairs on display, such as my wife slept with the whole of Wakefield, my husband slept with the whole of Wakefield, my cat stole the will money, and my three-year-old ethnic minority trans-species son burnt down the local church, it's no wonder none of you can be arsed to get off your sofa to do anything else!

The Jimmy Daniels Show: he shouts at smackheads for your entertainment.

Two

Rodney's stomach burned. After jumping to his death, he wouldn't have hoped he'd open his eyes again. He woke up in the sky, inside a ring of clouds. Rodney wasn't in Hell; Hell was inside Rodney. A gold beam of light burst through the clouds. He held a hand above his eyes to make out the figure emerging from the sun. Seconds later, a big hairy pair of testicles plonked down in front of him.

'GREETINGS, RODNEY. I AM GOD.'

'You're God?'

'Of course. Why wouldn't I be?'

'You're a pair of testicles.'

'And? Of course a pair of testicles made the world. What else do you think made it?'

'Honestly, I didn't give it that much thought. Though considering all the crap in the world, I shouldn't be surprised. You're kind of a dick.'

'I'm not a dick, Rodney. I'm a pair of testicles.'

'Same thing, really.'

'I'm more interested in why you think my world is crap. I can't help war and famine, you know.'

'Never said owt about them, did I? What riles me up is every day I have to wake up, go to my lousy job, get abused by entitled customers, then go home to a girlfriend who I can't stand. Over and over again. I had enough. That's why I left.'

Then God said to Rodney, 'You're a bit of a pussy, aren't you?'

'So?'

God let out an almighty tut. 'Noah had to build an ark for every animal on the planet. You don't see him complaining. Do you have any idea how long it took him to build an entire ark by himself?'

'Forty days, weren't it?'

'Don't be an arsehole, Rodney. Of course it took him longer than forty days. Not only did he have to build the ark, he had to travel the world to find two of every animal. Do you have any idea how long it took him to find two Fangtooths?

'He kept having to rebuild the ark to make up for the extra

amount of animals—in fact, he's still building it right now. It's hilarious to watch. Every time he thinks he's done, a new species of animal comes out. I bet he wishes he got it done back in the old days. Nowadays, there are too many regulations. The WWF lambasted him for animal cruelty after he tried to get a whale on board. The job's not without its danger either. Somali pirates nearly hijacked the ark when he tried to pick up some crabs off the coast of Mogadishu. My point is, if Noah can spend an eternity building an ark, you can work a lifetime at Burger Hole.'

'My point is, why is Noah building his ark?'

'To save himself when the flood comes.'

'Wouldn't it be a lot less stressful for him if he just drowned instead?'

God shook his balls. 'Oh, Rodney, you are miserable.'

'I know. That's why I quit Earth. I can't tell you how disappointed I am that there is an afterlife.'

'There isn't an afterlife, Rodney. You're not dead yet; you're in coma world. You're lucky Dante was a liar—you could be a tree right now. Anyway, I have a job for you, Rodney. I have an alternative world that needs saving. If you save it, I'll let you live in it forever.'

'No thanks. I'd rather die now.'

'Nonsense. You might find the fresh life invigorating. Oh, my eyes can see it now. This will be such an original story arc. You, the pessimist who killed himself, will begrudgingly accept this heroic burden I place upon you. You will soon meet up with the girl I have also bestowed this quest upon. Initially, you will dislike each other, but in time you will grow fond of one another's differences. Then there'll be a fallout over a misjudgement of communication, and the story will stop being funny and start being sombre. But in an act of glory, you will win her love back, and you will realise that life really is a cheery happy place after all! What do you say, pal?'

'Fuck off, God. I'm not doing that.'

'How about you just save the world, then?'

'No. I wanna die.'

'Tough. I need someone to save the world, and you are the chosen one because of lazy writing and all that. Besides, I've started a rumour that you had sex with a mongoose before you died. I can get rid of the rumour before it picks up momentum, but if you die now, everybody in the real world will wonder what you've been up to. Surely even you don't want to be remembered as the man who committed suicide because he had sex with a mongoose? Because that's what you'll be remembered for.'

Rodney sighed. 'Fine. I'll be your hero. What do you need me to do?'

'An evil group has overrun one of my worlds. They call them …*The unlabelled*—actually, they don't call them that, because the unlabelled throw a paddy if you give them any label, but for the sake of making it easier to refer to their group without having to go into valid detail every time, we'll label them the unlabelled. Anyway. I mentioned a girl before; you will need to work with her to get rid of the unlabelled.'

'Can't you just send a flood?'

'Everybody already hates me, Rodney. I don't need to give them another reason.'

'Okay.'

'I knew you'd come around, Rodney! Now I will send you to your new Earth.'

KAPOOF!

Rodney was gone.

Three

…then Noah said to the health and safety inspector, 'Come on, man. My boat's survived all this time with over a million different species on it. I'm not taking down an entire deck.'

Rodney arrived at alternative Earth. Right now, I have the chance to create a unique world, where there are fridges the size of mountains, where grass is orange, and where children pay money to use a toilet van instead of an ice-cream van. Instead, Rodney awoke on a bus, next to a girl who smelt like she had a dead rabbit hidden under her hoodie. He didn't dance around the subject. 'You smell like you've been violated by a skunk.'

'That's just the smell of the perfume I'm wearing. I'm trying to fit in with the unlabelled. They don't like the smell of regular deodorants or perfumes; they say they're too mainstream. They prefer the smell of roadkill and bowel problems. I'm Tara, by the way. You must be Rodney. God told me to find someone who looked like their face was about to fall off, and you fit the bill.' Rodney glared as they shook hands.

'Why are we on a bus? This doesn't make sense.'

'Does anything make sense?' Tara said. 'Think about it. Think about everything around you. Try to truly comprehend it all, and nothing makes any sense. Try to think why it is you see and hear things around you, why certain things or people make you feel happy or sad, and why is it we are not just emotionless voids going nowhere. It makes no sense. But someone will tell you, you feel this way because yada yada yada. But why yada yada yada? And why whatever the answer is to yada yada yada? What created the force that created the big bang, and why is it so ridiculous to believe anything, even a giant shoe, made the force, when everything is already so ridiculous? Why so hard to believe the world hatched from an egg one day? In a world where water falls from the sky, why is anything unbelievable?'

'That doesn't answer my—'

'It amazes me how so many people dismiss the idea that a god created the world, yet they accept Mars exists because the government says it's some rock you can see through a telescope.'

'Jesus pissing Christ,' Rodney moaned. 'I only want to know why we're on a bus.'

'Bit rude. Anyway, you're off to university. You've been enrolled on a creative-writing course. There, you should find a man who is close to the Unlabelled King. I have to do something else, so instead, there'll be a man you're very familiar with waiting to guide you. He'll tell you what you are going to do.'

A flashback of what God had said came to Rodney. *You will grow fond of one another's differences.* 'Oh.' He looked at Tara. 'Not being funny, but we won't be having a romantic relationship.'

'Wow, good job you started that sentence off with not being funny, otherwise I'd have laughed.' Rodney grunted. 'Relax, mate. I'm not bothered. You look like you've been dunked under a pool of vodka.'

Rodney growled. Little did he know that he would have the last laugh, because I kill Tara off in chapter seventeen (boiler alert, bro!).

Rodney got off the bus and looked at the new Earth. It looked exactly like the Earth he had come from (I'm not doing any describing, so if you want to know what Bradford looks like, Google it, though your imagination will probably give you a nicer image). He already felt annoyed about the new world (What? I haven't got time to *show* you how every character feels. Don't call me lazy. You work a full-time job and write a book at the same time).

He stood by the entrance to Bradford Hallam University or whatever the hell it's called. There didn't seem to be much difference in the new world, except there was a lot more sewage on the roads, buildings looked like they were going to collapse, and everyone looked a bit ill. Rodney recognised the man who pulled in beside him. He was surprised the familiar face didn't look ill. Johnny usually looked an ill yellow colour, yet now he looked like he'd just poured a bucket of tango over his face. He wore a baseball cap backward on his head. 'Johnny? What are you doing here? Did you try to die as well?'

'Nah, bro. Some girl called Tara told me that a version of you from another world would need my help.'

'Oh? What happened to the version of me in this world?'

'You what, mate?'

'I said, what happ—hang on a minute, what do you mean what?'

'I'm not made of ears, mate. I can't tell what you said.'

'Go back and read what I said, then.'

'Read what you said? What you on, Rodney? We're stood here having a spoken conversation. Why would I be able to read what you just said?'

'Never mind. What I said was, what happened to the version of me in this world?'

'You smiled, so everybody presumed something was wrong with you. After everybody kept asking you what was wrong, you blew a gasket and leathered a priest. You're currently sedated in an asylum.'

'Fair enough, I suppose. After all, I haven't laughed since 1996.' Rodney narrowed his eyes. 'You look suspiciously orange. Is that how Johnny looks in this world?'

'Nah, bro. I've just had some spare time.'

'Oh, aye. Booked time off work, did ya?'

'Nah, I got suspended. I picked up a second bookable offence after I two-foot tackled my line manager. I was already on a yellow for diving when I went to the printer.'

Rodney frowned. Alternative Johnny seemed annoyingly similar to the one from his own world. Real-world Johnny had once told Rodney that he had turned up to a job interview in a dressing gown—he claimed it made him look wise—then when asked to provide a referee, he brought his dad along to his job trial because he used to be a linesman at his junior football games. That wasn't surprising. This was the same man who thought a prostate exam was a GSCE science paper.

'Anyway, Rod. We better go do university stuff. We need the unlabelled to think we are one of them.'

Four

Rodney and Johnny sat down and waited for the marine-biology lecture to begin. The new equality act meant that every subject ever had to be taught to every student to give everybody the opportunity to be everything. The teacher entered the lecture hall and walked to the front of the room. He stood by a table which supported a fish bowl.

'Woof Woof!' he said. 'Herro, everyone. I'm Rofessor Dog. I will be your new teacher of rarine riology this year.' Professor Dog was a dog. He stood upright and wore a white shirt, but he was still a dog. 'Ranks to the rew requality ract by the rovernment, I, a dog, rinally rave the ropportunity to be a runiversity reacher.'

Johnny put his hand up.

'Yes, young man, rot would roo like to say?'

'I gotta ask, even though you're a dog, do you still know how to teach marine biology?'

'That's how the rovernment has rimproved things. Not only can I not teach you ranything of rany rimportance at all, but I can perform hilarious shenanigans to make your lessons rincredibly fun! Rike this!'

Professor Dog tapped the fish bowl with his paw. Suddenly, a fish jumped out of the bowl, wearing a pair of wide veiny eyes and a big grin.

'Hey, kids!' The fish shouted in a high voice.

For the next half hour, Professor Dog and the fish performed a musical number about marine bisexuals that ended in a fanatical climax of fireworks, elephants, and cabaret dancers. The students loved it so much that the lecture hall was flooded by bodily fluids, and several freshmen drowned.

Professor Dog dismissed the class.

'What did you think of that then, Rodney?' Johnny asked.

'I have no words.'

'You worried you won't get a good degree?'

'I'm not worried at all—'

'Actually, I don't know if you need a degree anymore,' Johnny

Yes, cactuses is a word. I even checked, so don't start with that cacti crap.

said. 'Not under the unlabelled government. It's frowned upon to be an expert in anything productive. Have you seen the jobs they've been giving to marine biologists? It's all about who can hold their breath under water the longest now. I don't think you need knowledge for that. In fact, I've got a hilarious video to show you.' Johnny led Rodney to a computer suite. 'Damn, there doesn't seem to be much room in here.'

Rodney pointed. 'There's a free space next to that black guy.'

'Woah, Rodney! I knew you'd be miserable, but I didn't know you'd be racist.'

'Racist? How's that racist?'

'Because you just called him a black guy.'

'But he is a black guy. Is he black or not?'

'Doesn't matter. You are not allowed to notice he is black. You are supposed to pretend you do not know what colour he is. By pointing out he is black, you are being racist.'

'But I didn't say any racist slurs. I didn't even insult him about the colour of his skin. I just pointed out that he is a black guy, because there is a free computer next to him.'

'Doesn't matter, still racist. You should have said there's a free space next to that African American guy.'

'We're in England. That doesn't even make sense.'

'Sense or no sense, bro. It's politically correct. Please consider your use of language in the future.'

Johnny sat at the computer beside the ~~black~~ African American guy. Rodney pulled up a spare chair and peeped over Johnny's shoulder. 'What was so great you dragged me in here for?'

'Do you remember that ex-football player who claimed to be unbeaten at everything?'

'No.'

'What, you don't remember Brad Steele? The same man who never lost a football game his entire career?'

'I'm not from this world. Why would I remember?'

'So you're telling me you don't remember Brad Steele? The same Brad Steele who went to space in a helicopter?'

'He went to space in a helicopter?'

'That's the guy! See, he was even unbeaten in the laws of physics.

Page 19. Coincidentally, 19 is the legal age for doing a poo in Slovenia.

19.

A bunch of jealous people tried to start a rumour that he'd taken a load of performance-enhancing drugs. Turned out his blood was so clean, they used it to feed third-world countries. Now watch this video.' Johnny put on a video titled Brad Steele Marine Biology Challenge.

Fish swimming.

'Marine biology. A job we associate with fish and the sea. Thanks to the new government scheme, that awful stereotype of marine biology can be replaced by fun and excitement. Instead of doing whatever the hell they were doing before, marine biologists now take part in fun games to see who can hold their breath under water the longest.'

Several workers gasping for air.

'The game was taken to a whole new level when the unbeatable Brad Steele took the challenge.'

Intense, jacked bald man.

'I'm Brad Steele, and I'm unbeaten at everything!'

Jacked bald man bench-pressing a concord.

'Whether it's kicking ass around the world or kicking ass in my living room against little weenies on *Call of Duty*—that's right, I ploughed all of your mums—I am unbeaten at everything! Now I'm ready for my biggest challenge yet! Being an unbeaten marine biologist!'

Jacked bald man lying face down atop the sea.

'Brad Steele took part in the marine-biologist underwater-breathing challenge. Unfortunately, Brad took the challenge so seriously he never came back up from the water and died. At least Brad will be able to rest safely with the fishes knowing that not only does he have a marine-biology record that will probably never be beaten, but he never lost at anything in his entire life.'

Johnny looked at Rod. 'Well?'

'That's the dumbest thing I've ever seen.'

'What are you talking about? That was hilario—oh crap. Here comes Trent.' Johnny sunk into his chair. A very big student entered the room, his two goons on either side of him. It was Trent Foot. He was the university football team captain, and he was number one on the jock world ranking. The two goons beside him, Tom and Tim,

If you count these pages manually by hand, you'll find they don't add up.

20.

looked like beefed-up versions of Rod and Johnny, which would be useful information if you had any idea what Rod and Johnny looked like. 'You better duck too,' Johnny whispered. 'He'll think you're the alternative version of yourself.' Rodney didn't bother.

Trent spotted Rod and Johnny. 'Well, well, well. If it isn't small Rod and rubber Johnny.' Tom and Tim chuckled at Trent's hilarious comment.

'Hey, Trent,' Johnny said, trembling. 'Tom, Tim. How you guys doing?'

'We need a computer so we can watch my mum in her new porn film. The only problem is this room is full of nerds, like you. There are no computers left. We want you to move.'

'Sure thing, Trent.' Johnny picked his bag up off the floor.

Rodney scowled at Trent. 'Maybe I'm comfy here.'

'Do you know who you're talking to, micro Rod? I'm the number-one jock in the world. I was even on the front cover of *The Jock Times*.' Tom held up a copy of *The Jock Times*, which indeed showed Trent on the front cover surrounded by naked ladies. 'If anybody has the power to push people around using their arrogance and size advantage, it's me. Now get off the computer!'

Johnny stood up. 'Come on, Rod. We better do what he says.'

Rodney squared up to Trent. 'Why don't you go ahead and kill me? See if I care.'

'Oooooooo! We got a tough guy here, boys. How about I give you a swirly, pencil Rod.' Rod grabbed Trent by the neck of his jacket. Tom and Tim immediately punched Rod in the stomach. Rod wheezed as he tried to get his breath. Trent gritted his teeth. 'Get the hell out of here, before I steal your lunch money.' Trent was serious now. He was serious before, but by pointing out that he was serious now, you are aware that he is, in fact, truthful that he would like to steal Rod's lunch money. Reluctantly, Rod and Johnny exited to the next scene.

Rodney and Johnny walked past a creative-writing board on the wall. It said:

Writing is about the freedom to use words however you want, but hold up—here are a load of rules on what you shouldn't do:

Don't substitute good writing for gimmicks.
No exposition.
Never end a sentence with a preposition.
Don't use a big word when a simple one will do the job.
Don't use random foreign words.
Never break the fourth wall.

'Would you like me to explain why the unlabelled have ruined the world?' Johnny asked. 'Shall I explain why, in as many words as is humanly possible?'

'No, I don't give a sh—'

'It started when the unlabelled government came into power. Initially, we were all fooled to vote for them. They said they could broaden our horizons, and we believed them. But we were wrong. Turns out the unlabelled are too cool to do anything. Ejemplo: There are no longer builders to rebuild the shoddy roads, because building is a trade that is too conventional for the government's tastes and has been banned. It shouldn't come as a surprise to anyone that God hates the unlabelled. After all, Eve was the original hipster. She could have just conformed like Adam, but no, she even looked down her nose at the Garden of bloody Eden. She just had to be different and bite the apple. I tell you, one of these days you'll see them all wearing nothing but leaves to cover themselves up. Would you like to know the heartbreak I have suffered, and why I personally hate the unlabelled?'

'No.'

'Well, I'll tell ya. My uncle had to go to the hospital to receive heart surgery. The unlabelled doctor said he would have him healthy in no time. But when it came to the operating table, the doctor decided heart surgery was too mainstream and gave my uncle a sex change instead. I remember the conversation they had when he woke up. "Good morning, Mr Parker." "Good morning, Doctor. Did you successfully unclog my artery?" "No, Mr Parker, but if you feel between your groin, you'll find your brand new vagina." And with that, my uncle had a heart attack. I vowed revenge on the unlabelled ever since.'

'Hopefully that will sink in,' Rodney said. 'That was all I needed to know about. Now I know why we must get rid of the unlabelled, it's time to move beyond.'

'Yes. We must fostaculate the unlabelled.'

'Gracias. Por Favor. Sentarse.'

Oh, by the way, make sure to keep up with all the new releases from me, Joseph Dawson, by following me on twitter @joedauthor1. Meanwhile, here's some more shameless promotion:

You've Been Framed…

Returning to ITV this winter, it's the cheapest form of entertainment ever made. It's *You've Been Framed…for Murder!*

Watch members of the public get recorded by home video cameras as we frame them for committing the most serious crime of all! Moider! HEHEHEHE!

'Now let me just reverse out of my dri—what was that bump? Who is that bearded man wearing a bloodstained shirt behind me?'

'Oh my God! That guy just ran over that child, who was in no way thrown under his car or dead already!' WEE WOO WEE WOO. 'Oh, here comes the police! How convenient!'

'What the?'

WEE WOO --Sir, you're under arrest for murder! -- WEE WOO

Watch as innocent victims suffer in jail for crimes they didn't commit!

'Googoogaga babababa!'

WEE WOO -- Don't play innocent, little baby Timmy! You may only be ten months old, but your fingerprints are all over that knife that killed that east end mobster. That's all the evidence I need, you sick freak. -- WEE WOO

It's 100% authentic entertainment, which is in no way staged by people who want to receive two hundred quid for sending in their clips. *You've Been Framed for Murder.* Coming this winter.

Five

…then Noah said to God, 'This ark's costing me a fortune to build, boss. You couldn't lend us some dosh, could ya?'

'I'm not Wonga, Noah. If you want money, you should go to a loan shark, la la, loan shark.'

Johnny and Rodney got on a bus. 'Look!' Johnny shouted. 'It's him. The messenger of the Unlabelled King.' Before Rodney could reply, God gave him super mutant power. When I said mutant, I actually meant to say mute. He could not use his voice to stop Johnny, so he had to run after him.

The driver drove the bus from the back seat because he wanted to look hard. Johnny followed the messenger of the Unlabelled King and a girl to the centre of the bus. He sat on the seat beside them.

The messenger liked to think himself ironic. He was so ironic that he wore a tailor-made suit and had a shaved head. The woman looked like the only person in the world who remembered what *Big Wolf On Campus* was.

The messenger looked at Johnny. 'Ironic, don't you think? The government implements an equality scheme to broaden our minds, yet the realms of society remain as dull as ever.' He was so contrarian that he even bad-mouthed his own party now that they were in power.

'Er, yeah. That's pretty ironic, I guess,' Johnny replied.

'My name is Phoenix,' the messenger said. 'Phoenix Hendricks. This is my girlfriend, Lavender Youth.'

'What a splendid triumph it is to meet you!' Lavender yelled. 'Man the cannon fodder, Gareth! Ha!' She was certainly more charismatic than Phoenix, but that wasn't very hard. Her reluctance to use normal human dialogue was absurd. She was like a disobedient bath, pouring water back into the tap it came from. 'Unicorns and spam fritters!'

Johnny squinted. 'I'm sorry, Phoenix. Is, err, Lavender okay?'

'Don't mind mwah! I'm just so random! Mega Lol. Backagaga!'

'We don't conform to everyday normal conversations,' Phoenix said. 'Words aren't maths, you know. We make our own language not constricted by logic or meaning. Yeah, we're nonconformists. What does your T-shirt say?' Johnny took off his hoodie so Phoenix could read the big red text printed on his T-shirt: Surfer Warmer 93.

'My mum bought me this top because it was cheap,' Johnny conceded. 'I don't think the text on it means anything.'

'Oh, I see. By no meaning, you mean the government system is meaningless?' Johnny took up the face of a gazelle. 'I get it, man. You're one of the superior ones like us. Your T-shirt proves it. Its message is so deep and meaningful. All three of us are surfers on warm water living in an intellectual paradise where we can see through the wretched status quo the government is putting everyone through. The rest are part of the majority in the cold ocean, drowning.'

'Er, yeah, something like that.'

'I wanna go swimming with dolphins!' Lavender shouted. She cackled as she tried to impersonate a dolphin.

'What did you say your name was?' Phoenix asked.

'Johnny. Johnny Parker.'

'Hmm. I see you are still a slave to your adopted name. You don't have to conform to your parents, Jonathan. Call yourself whatever you want. I only just changed my name a third time. Last year, I was called Hopeful Willows.'

'Last week, I called myself Raspberry Ninja Girl! Hashtag Lol, hah!'

Johnny fumbled around in his pocket; his ball sack was stuck to his thigh. He tried to distract the messenger by talking. 'So, Phoenix and Lavender. Why is it you hate the government so much?'

'The equality act is making everything fun. I think they're ruining fun and making it too mainstream. If they keep trying to make things enjoyable and free, everybody's going to conform and do those things. I used to have fun before it was cool. Now all the unwashed masses are going to come in and completely kill the fun scene. I think we need more office jobs. Do you agree with me, Johnny?'

'I must admit, the country will fall apart because everybody will be too busy having fun.'

'That's on point, Jonathan. But hey, we must play this safe. At least doing boring work is back in its rightful place in the underground. I suppose we're keeping doing actual jobs safe from the massive conformists to ruin. You're clearly an enlightened individual, Jonathan. I have a proposition for you. How would you like to join me and Lavender in the fight against the government?'

'But isn't the King the government? I thought you were his messenger.'

'You have a lot to learn, Jonathan. You see, being anti-unlabelled against the biggest unlabelled person in the world makes me more unlabelled than anyone. You see, Jonathan. We unlabelled are as two-faced as the rest. It is not about our party. It is about the individual in our party, which must be me. Now will you help us?'

'Sure, that sounds great.'

'Splendid. There's a rally coming up. Our group needs a few more people. I don't suppose you know anyone else who could help?'

'My friend Rod.' He nodded toward Rod, who was unable to argue. 'He hates conformists almost as much as me.'

'Great. Now, obviously, we'll have to meet up some time beforehand to discuss what's going down. We'll meet up with you and your companion when we're not busy. I have quite a heavy schedule coming up; I'm going to be busy reading a thesaurus in order to improve my word vocabulary. That might take me a few days to revise. Now, what would be the best way to contact you?'

'I have a mobile.'

'I'm sorry, Jonathan. I don't use a mobile. I think they're too materialistic. I'll send a raven to you instead.'

'Er, yeah, that's fine.' The bus reached its stop.

'It was great meeting you, Jonathan. I'll be in touch with you soon.'

Lavender did a star jump. 'Bye ber bab blay ber bah!'

'Yeah, see you both later.'

Six

Suddenly, Tara pulled up alongside Johnny and Rodney in a ~~black~~ African American car. 'Quick! Get in!' They did.

She drove maniacally to an abandoned toilet store. Johnny asked, 'What's the matter?'

'No time to explain.'

'Okay. That's fine.'

Seven

The trio looked out of the toilet store window toward a gym, where they could both see and hear a massive man of mass—probably the 'roided dude from chapter 4. He made sure to accompany every dumbbell lift with a grunt that the whole of China could hear. Making everybody in the gym aware of his tremendous feats of strength was apparently part of his routine for building muscle. If the casual gym-goers could have articulated their collective thoughts, they would have said, 'All right, I can see how much more weight than me you can lift. You don't have to grunt like a constipated duck, for fuck's sake. We get it; you're stronger than us.' Of course, this lack of understanding for testosterone-fuelled heaving sounds was what made them filthy casuals. Do you even no-carbs diet, bro?

Rodney introduced Johnny and Tara to each other. 'Why are you against the unlabelled?' Johnny asked Tara.

'Because God wills it,' Tara replied.

'Ha! God! What a load of bollock. Am I right, Rodney?'

Rodney shrugged. 'My long-time opinion was that the Bible was a load of bollock. Then I found out God literally is a pair of bollocks, so it all makes sense in a way. Maybe that's something people don't consider. They say so much evil in the world means there must be an absence of God. Yet they never consider God might just be a pair of testicles.'

'That's fair enough, I suppose. After all, God's got sick banter. Remember that time he nearly got Abraham to sacrifice his son? Imagine the look on Isaac's face when God said, "Lol jokes, it was just banter!"'

'Maybe he created the world so he'd have things to destroy. It's not that farfetched. Back before I lost my spirit, I used to love building towers of Lego. I used to love booting them down even more.'

'You might be wise to bite your tongue in this world,' Johnny advised. 'The unlabelled don't care much for God. In fact, many believers were slaughtered by smugness after making their religion known.'

Tara tutted. 'They're so ignorant. Don't they know God is omnipotent?'

'God can't get it up?'

'Omnipotent, you idiot. I know he is, and I know he has the fools under a spell. He must want people to doubt his existence.'

'But don't people who reject God go to Hell?' Johnny asked. 'Therefore, doesn't God basically decide who goes to Hell?'

'No,' Rodney said. 'There isn't an afterlife. God told me.'

'Maybe God only told you that to test you,' Tara said. 'Maybe he only said that to see if you would live a life of goodwill without the knowledge that you would go to Hell if you did not.'

'I just jumped off a motorway bridge and left my girlfriend to live alone because I couldn't be arsed watching a football match at my mate's house. If God wanted to test how much goodwill I have, he would have sent me to Hell already.'

'Maybe the bad thing you did was for the greater good. Maybe it was for a better cause, like helping us get rid of the unlabelled.'

'We have people who think like that back in my world; they're called extremists.'

'Extremists?' said Johnny. 'You mean like people who ride skateboards and drink nothing but cans of Monster?'

Tara gasped. 'God would never put his plans in the hands of anyone who had anything to do with any monster.'

'Maybe God doesn't know whose hands his plans are in,' Johnny said, rubbing his orange chin. 'Maybe he created the world and then buggered off. That way people can say he clearly doesn't exist, and he didn't create the world—which may be what he wants people to think, so he has an excuse to grill people in Hell.'

'He doesn't need moral justification to do that,' said Rodney. 'He's God.'

'But maybe he does need moral justification. After all, something must have created God. He too must be judged by someone. After all, isn't God just like a human? I don't know if this is accurate, but doesn't it say in the Bible that God jizzed all over space to create the Earth? Therefore, isn't he like man after all?'

Then, I read that back and decided my year-eleven RE homework was ready to hand in.

The slump hiding in the shadows of Rodney's brief sun of enlightenment came back to knock the enthusiasm out of his body. He sulked over to a toilet, instinctively pulled his pants down, grunted, and pulled his pants back up when Johnny laughed. Johnny stopped laughing when a bunch of men in suits entered the toilet store. 'Gentlemen, I knew you'd come,' Tara said, smiling.

'Who the hell are these guys?' Rodney asked.

'Rodney, Johnny, meet the corporate bigwigs.'

'Pleased to meet you,' all twenty corporate bigwigs said in unison. Each one held their hand out. Rodney reluctantly shook one and then realised all the other bigwigs still had their hands held out.

'Really?' Rodney moaned. 'I have to do this for every single one?' Tara answered by elbowing him in the side. Twenty *What's your names* and *How are yous* later, the introductions looked like they were about to end. 'Okay, Tara, can you tell us what this is about—'

'Would anybody like a drink?' Tara asked. The introductions continued.

'Ooh, I never thought you'd ask. I'll have a tea please, one sugar, no milk,' 'I'll have a coffee, decaf if you don't mind,' 'I'll have a storming cup of Bovril, love,' etc. Tara made the brews and came back into the room.

'Are we all bloody ready now?' Rodney asked.

'Not just yet,' said Tara. 'First, we have to make small talk about where we've travelled from and how long it took us to get here.' Twenty pointless anecdotes about roadworks, and ten shit jokes about parking later, the meeting actually began, at which point fourteen of the bigwigs left because everything important to them had been discussed. 'As me, Johnny, and Rodney all know, the unlabelled are a group who must be stopped. I have invited you bigwigs here today because I believe you share the same goals as us.'

'Yes indeed,' said generic bigwig one. 'The unlabelled government is losing us precious money. Their propaganda has led to a shortening of the workforce. Without a workforce, we have nobody to exploit to fill our banks to the rafters. We were hoping you could be of help to us.'

'What is it you need us to do?'

'Here's our plan,' said generic bigwig two. 'We need you to get this country's workforce back. To do this, we need you to do all the hard work. We need you to break your backs to get the thing we want, and we need you to be the ones to take the flack of all the people who are unhappy because of decisions we make. Basically, we need you to do absolutely everything. Then, once you have achieved our goals, we will come out of our string of never-ending meetings to be there when the media comes, so we can pose with our biggest smiles and claim all the credit and receive all the accolades as our names are glorified in the headlines. Unless, of course, everything goes wrong, in which case we will leave the world to shit all over you. How does that fair deal sound?'

'You sound a lot like a burger man I know,' said Rodney.

Explosion! The walls burst to smithereens. A blaze of fire and a wave of heat sped across the shaking room. The bigwigs were blown to pieces. Conveniently, the three named characters were the only ones to survive the explosion. 'Jesus!' shouted Johnny. He found a note on the ground once the smoke had faded.

'Hello, Jonathan. It's Phoenix. I hope you don't mind, but I'll be sending all my messages via grenade now. Thanks to George R. R. Procrastinator, ravens have become popular, which means I am contractually obliged to hate them. Anyway, old chap, that rally I told you about is sooner than I thought it was. In fact, it's in the next chapter, so be there.'

Eight

…then Noah eventually said to God, 'Sorry, pal, I can't be arsed building this ark anymore.'

Tara, Rodney, and Johnny joined Phoenix and Lavender in the crowd of uniquely dressed protesters by Halifax headquarters. Sperm with nooses around their heads were painted onto the picket signs. Rodney thought he knew what the unlabelled were protesting for. Now that he had his tongue back, he could unload his thoughts on the Unlabelled King's messenger. First, he had to suffer as Phoenix introduced him, Rodney, and Tara to several members of their movement. Just to be a pain in the arse, I'm going to give the next three characters the same name.

First was Ashley, a man who craved attention so much, he sped over to Phoenix as soon as he saw him with the new people. 'Hi! I'm Ashley. What's your name? Where are you from? What do you do for a living? I build energy efficient fuels for NASA, and I play in a postmodern hip-hop band.' Ashley would do anything to be in the spotlight. He'd stand there on the border of Switzerland in 1938 as the Germans rolled past, shouting, 'Hitler, wait! Come this way! Invade us, not Austria!'

'I work at Subway,' said Johnny.

'Awesome!' Ashley shouted. 'I eat sandwiches! Oh, I've got something cool to show you! Let me pull my pants down and do the helicopter!' Ashley pulled his pants down and whirled his willy around. 'Ha-ha! Look at my penis flying around everybody!' And the unlabelled all made merry and clapped as Ashley did the windmill. He was loving life.

'Hoot hoot. A healthy form of festivity,' laughed Phoenix.

Rodney tried to moan, but Ashley drowned everybody out by shouting terrible jokes. 'What's brown and sticky? A brown stick. Also, my massive brown cock. Look, see! Look at me whirl it around! Everybody, look and laugh at how funny I am!' And the unlabelled laughed at the loud man who thrust his nob in front of several people's faces.

Phoenix smiled. 'Such a lionheart.' Since Ashley was distracted—flashing his cock in front of everyone's faces—Phoenix introduced the trio to his next friend. 'Tara, Johnny, Rodney. Meet Ashley.'

'Please to meet you. I'm Ashley. And you are? Oh, that's right. Tara, Johnny, and Rodney.'

Tara said, 'Please to meet—'

'You as well? It is a good meeting, isn't it? What are you doing with us today?'

'We're here with Phoenix to—'

'Join us in our protest campaign?' There was little point conversing with Ashley; she'd guess what you wanted to say and do your talking for you.

Meanwhile, losing the eyes of his audience, Ashley began pulling people's pants down in a desperate attempt to recapture everyone's attention. 'Ha! Look! Look at how much bigger my willy is than yours! You may be a woman, but I'd probably have a bigger vagina than you! Oh, your willy is bigger than mine? I bet that yours doesn't grow much—mine's probably bigger than yours erect. How about another joke? What did the Irishman say to the Englishman? Oh mi Jesus, look how big Ashley's willy is! Look everyone, my cock is out of my pants! Doesn't that make me funny, witty, and likeable?' And the crowd's laughter confirmed that it did.

Rodney shook his head. He looked at Phoenix. 'What are we actually do—'

'Doing here today?'

Rodney glared at Ashley. 'I'm perfectly capable of finishing my own—'

'Dinner without my mum and dad having to cut my meat up?'

'How the hell was your prediction—'

'For the EuroMillions jackpot only one number off?'

Rodney gave up talking to the woman, which was timely because Phoenix's third friend came over. Phoenix introduced her. 'Everybody, this is Ashley. Ashley, why don't you introduce yourself to everyone?'

Ashley's gimmick was she had to make everybody 100 percent aware she was an atheist. 'Hey, I'm Ashley. My mum and dad named me Mary, but there was no way I'd allow myself to have the same name as a phantom woman who somehow managed to get pregnant without having sex. Do you think I am smart and cool for pointing out plot holes in a book people have been ripping to shreds for centuries?'

'Only the coolest!' Johnny said. 'Mind-blowing stuff. Come to think of it, I bet it was God who had it away with Mary. He just abused his power and said it was a miracle so Joseph wouldn't smash his face in.'

'Ha! God,' Ashley laughed. 'There is no god. If there was a god, bad things wouldn't happen in the world. Bad things like people who wear chullos in public. Oh, the ignorance. Where is your god now, I say?'

Rodney suddenly remembered keeping his head warm in winter. He had an argument. 'Have you ever considered that not everybody puts as much emphasis on looking—'

'Like respectable members of society?'

'No, Ashley, I wasn't going to say that. I was going to sa—'

'Save money on your car insurance, so you can put more money toward your holiday?'

'Ashley, will you please shut the f—'

'Footsie one hundred down because you're losing all your money on the stock market?' Rodney gave up trying to get a word in, again.

Ashley smiled as she looked around. 'I love these protests. It's like Christmas has come all at once—not that I celebrate Christmas, because I don't believe Jesus was born—not that I'd celebrate it anyway, because I believe every day is a gift, and I don't need to greedily devour wrapping paper for the next gadget or gimmick—except for the latest MacBook, because I must keep up with the times.'

Phoenix laughed. 'Don't we all.' He turned toward Rodney, Tara, and Johnny. 'Now that you have a taste of our culture, let us proceed.' He led them through the crowd, leaving behind Ashley, who was now weeing on people's legs to keep everyone's eyes fixed on him. Phoenix took them to Lavender who was stood directly in front of Halifax headquarters.

Rodney had to address what Lavender was wearing. 'Why do you have a goldfish bowl on your head?'

'I'm like a spaceman, ha!'

Rodney had no words.

'Come on, Rodney,' said Tara. 'I bet everyone thought the first man to wear trousers was weird. Today's conventions are just ingrained in your mind. Let's be honest, you were just about to admit you wear a chullo. You can't complain about anyone's fashion sense.'

Rodney let out a deep breath. 'I'm sorry, but she's wearing a goldfish bowl on her head.'

'It's abstract, dude,' said Phoenix.

Rodney groaned. 'You can't just wear a goldfish bowl on your head and claim it's abstract.'

'You're just bitter and narrow-minded. It makes Lavender her own individual.'

'Yes, because she's a lot different to that guy over there with the cake tin on his head, or that guy over there who's wearing nothing but a miniskirt and a pair of washing up gloves. I can see his nob every time the wind blows.'

Phoenix tutted. 'I knew by your silence on the bus the other day that you were a dullard incapable of expression. Are you sure his presence here is a good thing, Jonathan?'

Johnny put a reassuring hand on Rodney's shoulder. Rodney glared as his friend spoke. 'Don't worry, Phoenix. Rodney is just being ironic.'

'Okay, amigo. I suppose the configuration always pontificates the era of vulgaris. Yabanstrial. Ha-ha.'

'That doesn't even make sense,' Rodney said.

'Balderdash to your manmade rules, I say. Language is not maths, and words are not numbers. I'll use them whatever way I want.' Phoenix rubbed his chin as he studied Rodney. 'Here's a question for you. I want to really know if you possess the required individualism to join our hive. I ask you this: If a man on a chair falls out of the top floor of a one-hundred-foot-tall building, can he jump off his chair just before it hits the ground to save himself?'

Rodney was about to swear at Phoenix, when Tara spoke out of turn. 'Ooh, that's clever,' she said. 'You're saying the man has wasted his life feeding the corporation, and the only way to save himself is to take a leap of faith, away from the security of his office chair?'

Metaphorically, he is falling, and each foot of the building represents another year of his life. He has to risk it all to fulfil his life.'

Phoenix stared blankly. He looked at Lavender, who was busy licking the glass of her goldfish bowl. He looked back at Tara. 'Yes. That is exactly what I meant.'

Rodney pointed a finger at Phoenix. 'I think you're a charade.'

Phoenix sniggered. 'You would question my authenticity, just because you are too stuck in your northern narrowness? Let me tell you the difference between me and you. When you see a cow, what do you see?'

'A cow.'

'Exactly. But when I see a cow, I see an artist. I don't just see an animal chewing grass. I see a complex mind full of abstract thoughts, but it can't get them out. Most men just take cows for livestock. But what happens when the cows get bored of producing milk and start producing music instead?'

'OMG! What if they play their udders as flutes?' Lavender shouted. 'Cowabunga!'

'Wouldn't that be ironic,' Phoenix said.

'Ironic?' But Rodney's question got lost when Johnny opened his mouth.

'I know all about irony, bro. I once went to the hairdressers and asked for a four all over. Just for banter, I went back the next day and asked for a three all over. Then I went the next day and asked for a two all over. Irony or what, bled?'

Rodney shook his head. He looked around at the protesters and their sperm signs. 'So you're rallying for abortion, are you?'

'Bah!' scoffed Phoenix. 'You're very mistaken. We're obviously rallying against wanking.'

'Come again?'

'No thanks. It's wrong. Do you know how many sperm you kill when you selfishly whack off? MASTURBATION IS MURDER.'

'Hang on a minute. Why are we protesting outside Halifax headquarters?'

'We're protesting against wanking, Rodney. We all know what banks are full of.'

Cheap laugh and a round of applause.

Phoenix rubbed his chin (for the second time in the same chapter, no doubt). 'I have a proposition for you, Rodney. We have an interview with a news reporter arranged. Go on camera and argue for our cause, and maybe we'll accept that you are a free-minded spirit.'

Rodney wanted to say no. He looked at Tara and could tell from the look in her eyes what he had to do. Begrudgingly, he nodded in acceptance. (Of course he'd nod in acceptance. Why else would he nod?)

An hour later, Rodney and Phoenix stood next to the news reporter. The protesters had not coincidentally chosen the moment to start their chants. Those behind the cause so they could have time off work for pretending to strike had their own chants. 'What do we want?'

'Something that's hard to obtain.'

'When do we want it?'

'Not soon, because I like having an excuse for not going to work.'

'I'm live outside Halifax headquarters,' Debra Williams said, in the same tone of voice every news reporter ever uses. 'I'm here with Rodney Hargrove and Phoenix Hendricks, two of the leading activists for the Masturbation Is Murder campaign. Rodney, what is it you are rallying against?'

'We're having a moan about people who recklessly wank. Let me make something clear. Wanking is wrong. Do you know how many millions of sperm you kill when you selfishly pleasure yourself? Think of all the potential you flush down the toilet after you wipe your tainted load on your tissue paper. What gives you the right to kill another living creature like sperm? Sperm that could grow up to be police officers, firefighters, or doctors.'

'What about sperm that doesn't make it to the egg during sex?' Debra asked. 'Should people be condemned for their death?'

The question lit a fire in Rodney. The campaign did have a good cause. 'God yes. I didn't even think about that. Of course they should be condemned. Too many people clogging up the world. If more people didn't spread their jizz as if it were going out of fashion, we wouldn't be overcrowded, we'd be self-sustainable, and I wouldn't have to work at Burger Hole. In fact, never mind preserving sperm. Castrate every man and get rid of it altogether. The world is full of too many cu—'

'Of course we are not condemning sex,' Phoenix said. 'That is, if the purpose of it is to create.'

Debra put her journalistic spin on things. 'So you would rob people of something that is a natural pleasure?'

Phoenix scoffed. 'An animalistic pleasure. We are human beings, not animals. People must escape their narrow-minded ways and find other pleasures in the world. Why, sewing a scarf can be more satisfying than sex, and it isn't murdering anything.'

'Sex aside,' Debra said. 'all of this master debate raises the real question we all need to ask ourselves: When is it all right to wank?'

'Save for one exception, it is never all right to wank under any circumstance,' Phoenix said, making his view very clear. 'The only time it is all right to wank is when you have run out of Pritt Stick and you need to glue a picture of yourself to your grandma's birthday card.'

'There you have it, folks. You're a criminal if you wish to whack one out unless you fancy giving Nan a salty treat.'

Bang! Bang!

'All right! Break it up, folks!'

Rodney turned aro—

Crack!

Rodney and Johnny fell to the ground. They were put on their backs and handcuffed by a policewoman.

Progress Review

What do you think, sir?

'Mine eyes, Billy, mine eyes. Your prose reeks of unoriginality.'

I thought my book was unique.

'Good golly, I hope you're trying to fool me. The only audience this book appeals to is the lowest common denominator, people whose satisfaction counts for nothing. I'll tell you how mundane this tiny load of dribble of yours is. You've used the word *the* at least eight hundred-odd times already. Who has the patience to carry on after reading the same word over and over again? Not only that, but it's the same word that's used in every novel ever. Why does the word *the* have every author ever under a spell? Why is everyone too uneducated to use another word to link sentences? It's blooming lazy. Ah, I suppose I can't blame you, pitiful fellow. After all, you are a scrubber from the north of England. It's even worse that you're the product of this shallow age of the Internet. No wonder there aren't any wordsmiths around anymore, right, Joyful James?'

--_blagan ragan dagan pagan…_

'Blooming marvellous! Remind me to finger myself with a hardback copy of Ulysses tonight.'

Apart from cutting down on the word *the*, what—

'If I'm being honest, Billy, I wish you'd stop using *the* altogether.'

Apart from that, is everything up to scratch?

'Don't make me chuckle, Billy Bumhead. Quite frankly, everything you have written is vile—none worse than that blundering flanderized Johnny. All your characters are one- or two-dimensional. At least Tara has potential, if you can give her another trait than Bible basher. Yes, I want you to make her a strong, independent woman.'

How do I do that?

'Use your imagination, boy! Give her a backstory if need be.'

Suppose I could give it a try.

'Just remember another one of the hundreds of rules on how to write a book: Good characters define events rather than being defined by them. I read that on your precious Internet, so it must be true.'

Nine

You're reading a Christmas special chapter! What's that you say? You want to find out what happens in't main plot? Tough, you're gonna have to suffer through this gimmick chapter whether it's December or not—although let's be honest, Christmas adverts start in September.

Tara was reading a Christmas book to her six-month-old daughter, because I am establishing that she is a mother (and who better to illustrate motherhood than a father of none?). Tara did everything mothers do: she drenched her daughter's food in gravy, so her little one could still enjoy a succulent slab of steak despite her underdeveloped teeth; she let her daughter rest her tired, sweet head on't comfy airbag inside her car while she shopped; she put her daughter in't washing machine, so she could efficiently clean her and her clothes all in one go. Yes, she did all't stuff good mothers do.

Tara read to her daughter. '…and Santa Claus delivered presents to everybody who was good. He was an incredibly generous and loving man, if not—'

'Wait just a minute!' was't shout that accompanied window glass smashing apart. A bunch of venomous women broke in, surrounding mother and daughter. A woman called Moira ranted, 'Did you just say what I thought you said? Did you say Santa Claus was a man? Good gracious! And a mother, no doubt, making that statement to her daughter? What hope have women got when you so easily give in tut powers of man? Don't you see how harmful to society this story you're telling is? You are saying that man brings more happiness tut world than women!'

Moira elbowed Tara in't face and told Tara number two her own story: Magical Mrs Sandra Claus. 'Once upon a time, Santa and Sandra Claus travelled around't world, delivering presents. Sandra both set up and drove their sleigh because she was precise and organised, whereas Santa was a reckless, arrogant buffoon who thought just because he had a penis between his legs that presents would magically appear in every house without any hard work. And if you don't believe me that women make better sleigh drivers than

I bet you couldn't tell if that was an actual quote from Ulysses, could you?

41.

men, read some bloody facts. Throughout fiction, Santa has crashed his sleigh several times. Sandra has not crashed once.

'They arrived on't first child's roof. Santa gestured tut chimney and said, "Ladies first." Sandra was gobsmacked. "I beg your fucking pardon?" Santa stammered to reply. "I-I-I—" Sandra stomped her feet down. "You offer me to go first just because I am a lady? How bloody rude. I don't need your condescension. Now get your Lapland lump down't bloody chimney, you patronising git." Sandra saw Santa's cheeks glowing red and his lower lip quivering. She descended proudly after him because she knew she had put him in his place.

'On't carpet, he put down what used to be called Santa's sack, which was now called Santa's womb because wombs are much better at carrying things than sacks. He pondered like a moron as he glanced around with a bunch of presents in his hand. Sandra rolled her eyes and said, "It's not blooming rocket science, ya daft sod. Just scatter them all over't room." He did so, but nervously and constantly under her instructions, else he'd have just stood there gormlessly. Despite this, he still put presents in stupid places, such as in't fireplace which their boots had left in piles of snow—which he also managed to trail around't entire living room—and in front o't door tut stairs, so whoever entered first would fall face first on tut floor. Silly buffoon pulled his back trying to lift a wrapped-up washing machine. Our heroine warrior sighed and lifted it herself using her iron yield and ox-like strength. She was much better at putting out presents than him. She moved him out o't way as he whined and held his lower back and had a blooming nerve when he gasped, "Pass us mince pie please, love. I'm dying here."

"'Pass yer't mince pie? Pass yer't mince pie? How about I pamper your pillows and scrub your belly while I'm at it? Who do you think you are talking to? Do you think my best place is in't kitchen, you vile pig? You'd have women do your every whim while you do nowt? You think we're slaves to you?" "I only wanted a mince pie…" he lied. He most obviously didn't just want that. He wanted to prove that he controlled her. "Pass yer't mince pie, my bloody eye," she rightfully scoffed. "Get it yourself, you lazy bigot!" Santa whimpered, and not because of his back. Our heroine stood

Life tip: If you can catch flies with your tongue, you're probably a lizard.

42.

with a valiant eagle stare held high because she knew she had put him in his place.

'After *she* had done all't hard work, and't presents were set, Santa pulled beside her with his pathetic wet face and wrapped his clumsy arms around her goddess body. He'd really done it now. HE WAS HUGGING HER. Sandra heroically shoved him off in defiance. "What on Earth! Do you think you own me? Are you trying to make a point that I am your property? By cradling me, do you wish to belittle me and treat me as a pet?" "I just wanted to warmly embrace my wife," Santa blatantly lied; he wanted to prove that she was his property. She shot him down. "Don't patronise me with that twaddle, you chauvinistic arse crack. You're just trying to put a cage around me. Now pull your pants down, go sit in't corner, and think about what you've done, young man." Santa lowered his head and followed her orders. She looked on proudly, at presents she had laid out, at a victory for Moira's movement.

'All was great because of Sandra Claus. She could rest easy, knowing she had done't next generation of heroines proud. And when little girls o't world opened their presents, they didn't receive any toys they asked for, because Sandra knew they were *man*made items designed to brainwash them. Instead, they were given pepper spray to defend themselves against't catcalling builders.'

Moira finished her story and felt proud of herself. Tara joined Moira's movement, a character trait that won't be covered again in this book (in other nonrelated news, my quest not to use *the* has come to an end. Quite simply, I can't be arsed).

Meanwhile, let's see what the media had to say about this chapter:

'Wow! This is the deepest Christmas story written since Dickens! Never mind an undigested bit of beef; I just had an entire bowel movement!'—*The Times*.

Ten

Rodney and Johnny waited in their cell at the police station. I very much doubt they would let two friends share the same cell, so for storyline purposes, let's say there was an outburst of asbestos in the other cell.

Elsewhere in the police station, an underage Huddersfield Town fan who had mouthed off at a steward for not letting him in when he was clearly drunk off his tits was getting treated to a curry by the police officers. Let's assess the fairness of that situation: he was getting a chicken tikka masala in a nice warm cell for threatening behaviour, while the Huddersfield faithful had to watch their team lose one-nil to Bury, a place represented on the map of England by a big flaming turd on a plate. The same hooligan would commit arson once he was released, hopeful he might get a free donner kebab out of it.

Rodney caught Johnny smiling out of the corner of his eye. To be fair, he didn't have anything else to look at, so he might have just been looking at Johnny rather than having to catch him with the corner of his eye. I once tried to catch a Frisbee with the corner of my eye to impress a girl. Meanwhile, I just found out Frisbee is spelt with a capital *F*—cheers, spell checker. 'Why are you so happy?' Rodney asked.

Johnny grinned. 'I can't believe we're in prison. Think of the hall of bad men we're now a part of.'

'Bad men? There's a fourteen-year-old out there getting a caution for stealing a traffic cone and putting it on his head. We're hardly in prison. We'll probably be back out in the public soon.'

Johnny rubbed his hands together. 'Just think, Rodney. Everyone's gonna think we're well hard now. How long do you think they'll give us? Oh, I hope we get a life sentence. We'll be right gangsters by the time we get out.'

'Do you know what a life sentence is?'

'Sure, bro. It's when you get sentenced for life and end up leaving jail four years later.'

Knock-knock.

DYK? Most people actually believe being shat on by a bird is good luck. How come they're not all smeared in bird poop all the time, then? **44.**

Johnny couldn't contain his smile. 'Ey up, here comes da heat.'
The same policewoman who had arrested them burst through
the door. 'GET DOWN! GET DOWN!' She pointed her gun.
Johnny shrieked and jumped on the floor. Rodney didn't bother
moving. 'False alarm. I thought I heard a murder going on. My crime
impulse is always tingling. Now then, boys, my name is Officer
Nancy, and I'm—argh! What the hell's that on your foot!' Nancy
pulled the trigger. Johnny screamed as the bullet just missed his toe.
'I GOT YOU, SUCKA!'

'Are you mentally cleared to be a police officer?' Rodney asked.

'Did you not see that ladybird on his shoe? It was about to mug
him—or worse! It could have knifed him.'

'What's it gonna do? Rob his shoelaces?'

'Never turn a blind eye on an insect. I slapped cuffs on a spider
last week for breaking into a house. The little bugger just stood there
like it owned the place, though the coward tried to run every time I
went after it—a sign of guilt if ever I've seen one. Don't even get me
started on bees. Always stealing plants from my garden. Keep a
vigilant eye on anything that is ~~black~~ African American and yellow.'

Johnny got back to his feet, now that the ground was soaked in
his urine. Rodney asked, 'Why were we arrested?'

Officer Nancy held her hands up. 'My bad. I saw your picket
signs and got you lot mixed up with the infamous sperm snatcher.'

'The sperm snatcher?'

'Indeed. There's a man going around pickpocketing people's
sperm. Men get asked for directions; next thing they know, their
pants are stained in jizz. The guy responsible has them stored in
secret labs across the country. We think he's mutating them. In the
meanwhile, you might wanna wear these.' Officer Nancy held up
what looked like a pair of latex undergarments.

'What are those?' Rodney asked.

'These are condom underpants—designed to stop your sperm
from spreading.'

Johnny grinned once more. 'I'm more accustomed to letting
people in my pants, not out of them. I don't need a cage fo—'

'PUT THE CONDOM UNDERPANTS ON NOW AND
SAVE YOUR SPERM!' Johnny trembled and took the underpants.

Officer Nancy turned to Rodney. 'You'll be all right, I bet. You look like the type of man who's already killed all his sperm with excessive drinking.' Johnny laughed. Nancy grabbed his lips. 'What was that?'

'Geesh,' he strained to say. 'I only laughed.'

'Oh. I apologise. Ever since I found out *manslaughter* and *man's laughter* contain the same letters, I have taken every male chuckle with a hint of caution. Beware. That fact may save your life. Anyhow. Your folks are waiting outside for you, boys. You best get going. I've got crime to attend to. I've just received news there's a wasp holding school children hostage inside an IT lesson.'

The two joined their ka-tet outside the police station. Now that Phoenix trusted Rodney and company, he took them to see the Unlabelled King, but not without being as energy efficient as possible. To save fuel, he pushed Johnny to their destination in a wheelbarrow, Lavender did a mad chain of forward rolls, Tara travelled via lion, and Rodney travelled via treadmill. How the fuck he got anywhere by travelling on a treadmill, I don't know. Rodney asked why they didn't travel via the teleportation system that existed in the alternative world. Unfortunately, customs for teleporting was a pain in the arse. Nobody ever considered that terrorists could teleport from one place to another.

They arrived at the national abstract art museum. Rodney wasn't at all surprised that this was where the Unlabelled King lived. 'Follow my lead,' Phoenix said. 'We can't let the King know I'm secretly trying to take his chair. The protest was for his benefit, *comprende?*'

Inside the NAAM (there is no joke there about 1986 Indian film *Naam*, if you're trying to find one) lived all the artwork of the modern mind. There was a slab of tarmac covered in chewing gum, there was a fishing rod in a vase, and there was an empty coat-hanger stand with a bunch of coats piled at the side of it. There was even a crowd gathered around a middle-aged woman rubbing herself in moisturiser. Above her, the sign read 'the lost art of putting cream over your eczema.'

'How is rubbing cream on yourself art?' Rodney moaned.

Johnny shrugged. 'Eczema has its perks these days. I heard that if you lose your job, you get given E45 cream.'

'You get given your P45.'

'Whatever the cream, bro. At least getting made redundant becomes something to look forward to.'

Rodney scouted the room some more. He was lost for words at the sight of a banana skin on top of a Christmas tree that was wearing a pair of sunglasses. His brain hurt at the sight of a paperclip sat on a chair. *'How is that art?'*

'The art of sitting down, bro,' Johnny suggested. 'Maybe you're supposed to sit on it. Maybe how you react to sitting on a paperclip tells you what kind of man you are.'

'Maybe the paperclip represents the metaphorical 'paperclip' that holds together the foundation of society, or in this case, the wooden chair,' Tara said. 'After all, paper does come from wood.'

'That theory would have substance if paperclips were made of paper,' said Rodney.

Tara shrugged. 'Maybe there's a history about the paperclip that makes it fascinating.'

'Hardly bloody likely. It was bought this morning from Staples. I can see the receipt sat next to it,' Rodney pointed out. 'That is not art.'

'I agree with you, Rodney,' said Phoenix. Rodney didn't know what to make of Phoenix agreeing with him. He remained wary of his opinion. 'How can these objects be classed as art? They are nothing but ugly clutter to the world, just like paintings and sculptures.'

'What's wrong with paintings and sculptures?' Tara asked.

'Paintings and sculptures are physical objects that waste space. I prefer real art that doesn't waste the world's resources, like the unique craft of breathing in and out, or imagining that you are an atom in a speck of dust.'

'Why did I almost think for a moment we were on the same wavelength?' said Rodney.

'Ooh, wavelengths. That's good virtuosity, man.'

'Why does it matter if art is physical or conceptual?' said Tara. 'Does it matter what art is as long as it means something to someone? To me, art is anything that makes you feel.'

'Wrong,' Phoenix scoffed. 'All the ugly manmade buildings that they give the fancy name 'architecture' make me feel, yet I would not call them art, because what they make me feel is disdain. Gothic,

Victorian, or modern, they are ugly. I hate living in this artificial world.'

'Go live in the fucking woods, then,' Rodney shouted.

Among all this, a very bossy man was trying to yell the museum down. Ed Boner yelled both at staff what to do and at customers what not to do. 'Don't you step over that line! Oi, you, go check security! Excuse me, ma'am, would you please not breathe on that bronze centaur?'

Ed Boner's favourite band was Blink-182. His love for them was a secret because God forbid he listen to anyone other than Arcade Fire—hang on, Arcade Fire won a Brit Award didn't they? That's them off the playlist. Time to find a new band.

Ed Boner spotted Phoen—

'Oh my.' Ed's eyes bulged out of their sockets. He quickly opened a nearby cupboard and pulled out a vac. He ran to Rodney and vacuumed his face.

When he got his face back—after the suction had left a red ring on his face—Rodney said, 'What the hell, you jebend.'

'Your face needs lifting,' said Ed. 'You're putting a damper on this aesthetic paradise.'

'I swear on me mum—'

Phoenix placed a hand on Rodney's shoulder. 'Relax, Rodney. That's just Ed Boner.'

'Ed Boner? Ha,' said Tara, laughing.

Ed figuratively jumped on her back. 'What's it to you? I'll have you know, the Boners come from a respectable family lineage. My great-grandfather invented sitting down.'

'Funny, I'd have thought he'd have invented standing up.'

'No, I said sitting down, you dumbo. Who do you originate from, huh?'

'God. You know, that guy who created the world? And upon failure of his existence, I came from the first fish that evolved into man, just like everybody else.' Tara wore a proud grin on her face after that one.

Ed shook his head. 'It never fails to amaze me when you mouth-breathers pretend to be smart. What reasons do you have for bringing their kind here, Phoenix?'

'We're here to see the King after our protest. Can you take us to him?'

Ed happened to be one of those people who answered questions by asking questions. 'What have you done now? Why do you need to see the King?'

'I must introduce him to our newest members. Is he here?'

'Why wouldn't he be here? Are you suggesting something happened to him?'

'Not at all. You know I know the King can look out for himself, right?'

'Are you saying that I know that you know the King can look out for himself because you wish for him to walk without security so you can get him? Is that what you just asked?'

'Oh, for God's sake,' Rodney interrupted. 'Take us to see him.'

Ed snarled. 'Very well. But, I am only taking you to see him because of your work at the protest. *Not* because you asked me to.'

Onward, Ed led the group to the King of the Unlabelled. Phoenix gave a final warning before they entered the King's chambers. 'Whatever you do, do not call him the Unlabelled King.' Yes, you are correct. One of them is obviously going to call him the Unlabelled King.

They entered the King's chambers. The man himself was sat in the middle of the room. The throne he sat upon was a potty, so he could dwell on, glorify, contemplate, and commiserate his shit as it left his body. He wore the following: a crown that looked like a supersized sock, a robe of daffodil petals, and a moustache with a hundred little twirls.

As soon as they were close enough to hear him, it was clear he had some kind of staff dilemma. 'Now, who should I sack?' the King said to a messenger beside him. 'Dorothy Whatmore? No. Junior Cannister? No? Ali Hassan? Yes, sack him. Ah, Phoenix and Lavender, my old chums. Your debarkation is a most congenial one.' Phoenix was glowing. Rodney could see how impressed he was by the King's thesaurus-reading skills.

'Jeepers, King!' Lavender barked. 'Let me doo-ron-ron with my wife. I'm bi. Let me do drugs. Lol, jokes. I'll just do loads of coke. Cola, that is, ha-ha. Then I can be high sexual.' The Unlabelled King performed the strangest laugh to her 'quirkiness.' His big mouth chattered up and down, yet no sound came out of it. He looked like a chain chomp having a stroke.

'Oh, such a delightful creature,' the Unlabelled King said. 'Always one to rouse the spirit. You have brought guests.' Johnny bowed down to the King. Rodney glared at his friend, then lifted his head and saw the King studying him. 'You are the one who made the broadcast on television?' the King asked Rodney.

'Yup.'

'Splendid! You did a sterling job. One moment, please. Who else can I send to the metaphorical guillotine? Rory Lionfodder? No. Phillestine Garland? No. Ah yes, Rajid Malik. Off with his head! Back to you, chum. Rodney, isn't it? You made our congregation proud.'

'What exactly did I do?'

'Why, you helped us keep the divide. We need the divide; it gives us something to ridicule, so we can make ourselves look intellectually superior to everyone else.'

'Why does that help you?'

'Because there is nothing more satisfying than a good old grandiloquent moan. Don't be mistaken; when you moan, you are being a narrow-minded dimwit, but when we moan, we are being rebellious free spirits. Do you know why the world celebrates me for being revolutionary? Because I have the outlet to berate anything that gains a following and turn the public against it through superficially grandiose propaganda. The country is in my hands, and I have the power to make whatever I want popular before everyone moves on to the next thing like the mindless sheep they are.'

Tara stomped her foot down. 'You're the media!'

'Well, yes. I am the government.'

'This society of smugness is your fault. I shan't stand for this. I will out you to the world.'

'The news of the world thinks I am a Renaissance man,' the Unlabelled King said, laughing. 'Good luck with that.'

'There are always ways to turn the people against you,' Tara said.

'Do you know my true power? You see, long ago—ten minutes ago, actually—I was blessed with an ability. I have the ability to feed off the smugness of society. When smugness reaches high levels, I have the ability to do anything to anyone. Luckily for you, smug levels are low. It is why I am sacking people, to create airs of grievance. Speaking of which: Foxflick Winklepicker? No. Kingsley Oxford-Barriston-Thauvin? Oh gosh, never. Mohammed Hussein? Get him to the jobcentre!'

Tara shook her fist. 'It'll be a cold day in Hell before I let you get away with this.' She stomped out the room.

'The centre of Hell is cold according to Dante, you arsewipe,' the King shouted. 'Choose your next move wisely. The public divide the wank campaign has caused will create more smugness. I warn you, my true power will come.' He considered the other four. 'As for you cretins, get out of my sight. I never want to see you again.'

Phoenix gasped. 'But my King—'

'I read what you said earlier on in this chapter, Phoenix. You organised that protest to create a conflict that would make me look bad, not to create a conflict that I could be the people's leading protestor for. Good day to you.' The four followed Tara out of the national abstract art museum. The streets were full of Asians throwing their ties up. The front pages of tomorrow's newspapers were already set with a picture of the Unlabelled King, and a quote of him saying, 'We need to stop racist businesses sacking people because of their skin colour.'

The Gorilla Who Lost His Underpants

Buy Billy Crevis (aspirin or-fur)

"Come again?" said Reginald, and I did, all over his face.

Non-related killer first line aside...

...would be a terrible football match.

Gorgonzola the Gorilla felt like how Julius Caesar would have felt if Julius Caesar was an angry gorilla who had just lost his underpants. It couldn't have come (all over his face) at a worse time. Gorgonzola had just won the Nobel Peace Prize for being the first gorilla to commit to the grueling schedule of a 9 till 5 office job. The effort gone towards putting on his shirt and tie was all for nothing if he couldn't find his pants—how could he possibly look like a respectable gorilla?

Calmer days, Gorgonzola. Calmer days. Think of the bowling alley.

Gorgonzola used to love going to the bowling alley and urinating in all the bowling balls. The place hadn't been the same since PETA launched a campaign for the sexual rights of bowling bowls. Now, you're no longer allowed to stick your fingers inside a bowling ball without its consent, which is hard to get, because contrary to popular belief, bowling balls can't actually talk.

Let's go present tense. Somewhere in the world—aka America, because as Hollywood has taught us, America is the only place that matters—right now, there is a kid at a birthday party chatting shit about how he's the best bowler in the world. He mocks everybody who doesn't get a strike, then when it gets to his turn, he uses the ramp and gets a strike, then brags like he's Billy big bollocks. This same kid will be walking down the street when a flustered gorilla in a shirt and tie shouts in his face, 'Have you seen my underpants anywhere?' The kid won't have time to tell the gorilla his underpants are on his head, before the gorilla runs offs.

Unfortunately, the kid has chatted so much shit for so long, nobody will believe him when he tells them what he has just seen. Things the kid has chatted shit about:

- My dad lets me drive the car to school.
- I once swam from England to France.
- I used to be ball boy for Barcelona, and one time, they subbed me on when they were drawing, and I scored the winner.
- My brother works for Al-Quade, and if you don't let me play on your PlayStation, I'll get him to blow you up.

The kid couldn't get anybody to believe he had seen a gorilla in a shirt and tie, but he could write a story about it. His handwriting looked just like Calibri font.

GRILLA IN A SHIRT AND TIE

Once upon a time there was a really cool kid who was me and I was really popular and I had 800 trillion dollars in my piggy bank. I had just gotten my blackbelt in being a ninja when I saw a grilla down the road and it was ripping peoples arms off and it was poking people up the bumhole and it smelt like eggy farts.

The police were so scared they rang 999 and I answered my phone and I said "hello" and the police said "help us Dillon! You are the only one strong enough to stop the grilla!"

I am really really fast and strong and I ran to Paris in 2 seconds and I picked up the Eiffel tower and hit the grilla over the head with it. I crushed the grilla but then suddenly it turned into a bazillion mini grillas and they started running up peoples legs and hiding in their bumholes. One by one by two divided by six I put my finger up everybodys bumhole in the world and pulled out the mini grillas and crushed them with my pinky finger. Sometimes I was too strong and accidently pulled out peoples intestines but it was a small reward to pay for what I had done.

All of a sudden the grilla with the shirt and tie took off his invisible powers. He had been hide all along.

To make sure he didn't trick me again I went to the sea and picked up all the water in my mouth then poured it all over the grilla so he drownded.

Then I was declared president of the universe and Nintendo created a game series called the Legend of Dillon.

Unfortunately for Dillion, he chatted more shit and tried to pass his story off as something that had actually happened. At the end of his story, he put

By David Atimbura

confident that would trick people into believing he had picked up the world's biggest tower and had hit a gorilla over the head with it. What gave away Dillion's story as bullshit was nobody recalled him sticking his fingers up their butt. What also gave away Dillon's story as bullshit was that Dillon had written it, and Dillon chatted shit.

Nevertheless, there was one bit of truth to GRILLA IN A SHIRT AND TIE: There was a gorilla in a shirt and tie... And a pair of underpants on his head.

Dillon wrote the same story at school for what he did over the weekend, except the letters q, x, and k were replaced by cw, ecs and c (not entirely true, because there was never a q in Dillon's story), which was wise on Dillon's part because there's no reason for those letters to exist.

Dillon's teacher, Miss Shobss, had her own uniqueness when it came to the alphabet. Rather than using the phonetic alphabet to signify letters when on the phone, she had her own array of words.

"And what name does the account come under?"

"Miss Shobss."

"Shobss—and how do you spell that?"

"Shobss: S for syntax error, H for halibut crab, O for orthopedic diagram, B for Bognor Regis, S for syntax error, and finally, S for scrotum up my nose."

Miss Shobss didn't like being a teacher and only worked in a school because she liked to eat pencil shavings, and kids who loved to go mental with a pencil sharpener were the best source of such thing. Miss Shobss was always disappointed when she went out to a restaurant.

"Would anybody like some mozzarella on their dish?"

"No thanks, but do you have any pencil shavings?"

They never did, and Miss Shobss always had to bring her own pencil and sharpener. It was discrimination that they didn't meet her needs, no matter how absurd her needs were; as far as the unwritten consumerism act was concerned, if your customer wanted to eat their dinner out of the chef's grandma's arse, you better bring her along and lay her on the table.

Miss Shobss skipped through the children's work as she marked it. She gave Dillon's Grilla story the same treatment—until she read about the Eiffel Tower. Miss Shobss was a major conspiracy theorist. If Dillon could pick up the tower, it proved what she already knew—

the Eiffel Tower was just a big inflatable balloon created by the illuminati.

"I knew it!" Miss Shobss shouted. "Just like I knew the moon landing never happened—the moon doesn't even exist."

Miss Shobss also though that night time was a concept created by the government to get people to pay for electricity. She also thought the Irish were actually a bunch of eggs with faces drawn on—at least she was right about that one.

Miss Shobss rang the French.

French people are notorious for being very nosey, so when one person's phone rang, every French person in ??? (France or the world?) answered the phone. "Oui?" said every French person.

"Oui?"

"Oui? That's how you spell it? Not wi?"

"What are you talking about? You'll soon be telling me you don't use Oui-Fi. What is it you want Miss Shobbs?"

"I have just found out—"

Miss Shobbs cut herself off. She heard *him* enter the phone call. The French were quiet—except one.

It was the French President, Pierre Monte. Monti was a very arrogant man and had a résumé for being perfect. He was both a very smart and a very smart. He became French President at the mere age of eighty-six. He previously worked as a model, and at the age of ninety-one won most tanned penis. Despite being the French President, Monti wore a stylish crop top, a pair of gloves on his feet, and a pair of feet on his mum.

"You do not fool me, Miss America!" Monti yelled. "It is obvious why you are calling! I know you filthy

American's and your lust for power. America is clearly looking to seize an opportunity of some sort, but I will have all the power! Because we all know, with great power comes a great amount of poontang!"

"Mr Monti, I can assure you that I am doing this for the future benefit of mankind," said Miss Shobss. "We could be upon catastrophic changes in the world."

"I don't care who you are or what you stand for! The USA should not be considered anything more than a practical joke with citizens like you! How can you have knowledge of war and economics, when you are not even focused right now? You are too busy thinking about touching yourself over my hot body and tanned penis!"

However, Pierre Monti's comments were a mutual bluff; he was the one thinking about Miss Shobss in a pair of nipple tassels and a bin liner over her head. If he'd have stood up from the table, the whole of France would have seen his rock-hard erection.

On the other hand, Miss Shobbs was thinking what it would be like to be a caterpillar that had boobies. When she finished on the phone with Monti, she wrote what would become the bestselling story in the erotic romance genre:

The Caterpillar That Had Boobies

They're once were a caterpillar that had a big bulging pair of double d's. She wasn't like all the other caterpillars; she were special, but none of the others could see it. She tried to fly like all the other caterpillars, but her big jiggly boobies weighed her down. All the other caterpillars laughed at her and threw cornflakes at her. The Caterpillar was allergict to cereal and got cataracts. But her problems were gone whenever Sir Tristam Grey the caterpillar came along. He was so beautiful and his penis was so big that his mere presence cured her cataracts. She wrote about him in her diary:

I ooze a sea of ecstasy for Sir Tristam Grey, like an eagle doing a wee in the ocean. My inner goddess squirms with giddy pleasure, as he rubs me from my BBQ-flavoured North American brown-eyed goddess to my scraggy isthmus, like a European miner poking around in there. Tristam and my inner goddess are having their very own penis war. I ooze with ecstatic anticipation, like when you've been holding a poo in for four hours and you finally get to go to the toilet.

The caterpillar couldn't fit in a cocoon because her boobies were too big. All the other caterpillars laughed and hit her over the head with a sugar puff. Super sexy Sir Tristam Grey swooped down and kissed her on the lips. The caterpillar instantly became a butterfly and her boobies grew thrice the size, and all the other butterflies saw how beautiful she really was because of her massive boobies, and it was all thanks to Sir Tristam Grey and his beautiful face and his 16inch penis.

Pierre Monti would never have concerned himself with Miss Shobbs story. Pierre had his own interests. Today was the day of the Nobel Peace Prize. It was a big night for Monti. Not only were France hosting the prize to the first ever gorilla winner, but it was a chance for Monti to edge closer to fulfilling a lifelong dream. Ever since he was a little boy, Monti had dreamt about sharing a bath with a gorilla. All he had to do was seduce Gorgonza. He knew it would not be an easy task. No. Not like humans, who were instantly seduced when he showed them his tanned penis. No. He would have to throw more than his golden todger at the gorilla.

To make sure Gorgonzola the Gorilla had as pleasant a stay in France as possible, Monti decided to ban ugliness. This was a hard decision for Monti because it meant he had to get rid of the vice president, Snail McFroglegs, who had nipples for eyes.

So it was that Snail McFroglegs was exiled from France and forced to live on the mean streets of Luxembourg.

Snail McFroglegs was fuming. He was angrier than someone who's just been poked in the eye with a willy. He couldn't keep his anger to himself. The mean average streets of Luxembourg were about to become a whole lot meaner.

Snail McFroglegs had a cunning.

But before I can tell you that story, we must go back in time…

"How's your garden doing?" Clarissa said to me.

"Not good," I screamed in her face. "It keeps sniffling and it sounds very hoarse. I think it's coming down with something."

"That's too bad," Clarissa said. "Anyway, how's your garden doing?"

"Looking pretty good thanks," I said. "We're letting the grass grow completely out of control, while we've also sprayed attractive pesticide so all the local cats come over and take a shit in it."

"Cracking flags!" Clarissa shouted. "Where did you get such a good idea?"

"Well, my great-grandad used to glue grass to his back, so I've always been in love with the stuff. As for cat shit, I like to put it in envelopes and post it through my neighbours' doors, with a note saying 'Your cat forgot something in my garden. Fear not, I have returned what is hers ;)'

Then I got a lecture for assuming the cat's gender. Then I got a lecture for assuming it was a cat at all. I was ridiculed by the national papers for being racist against cats.

To let off some steam and forget about this humiliating disaster, I booked a pedicure at the local farm. First, I had the first ever horse pedicure and the horse ate my face and it was really nice. Then, they laid me on a table and put cream on my face and a towel on my head. They did not have any cucumber, so instead, they slaughtered a pig and put two pieces of salami over my eyes and it were well good. Then I was naked and Farmer Giles gave me a massage, but I was so excited that I did a poo and got kicked out.

Now that you know the backstory, we can continue with our original quest...

To save money, the government and the NHS had teamed up to employ No Nonsense Nelly's around the country to help people with any kind of problem. Gorgonzola the Gorilla still couldn't find his underpants, so he went to his local No Nonsense Nelly. Nelly was in her no nonsense mode as usual. "Next."

"You've got to help me, Nelly. I think I've got depression and I'm going to kill myself."

"Depression? Bah! That's the bloody puberty talking."

"But, Nelly. I'm Fifty-Two."

"Bloody laziness talking, then. Same reason why you're not killing yourself. Next!"

"Nelly, you have to help me claim benefit from the government."

Nelly groaned. "Go on…" Her patient lifted his arms up and revealed two stumps where his hands should have been. Nelly wasn't impressed. "Go on…"

"My work place never showed me how to use the buzz saw properly. I didn't know what I was doing, and my hands got stuck in there and the buzz saw took them straight off."

"Oh aye, here we bloody go again. The old, 'I got my hands stuck in a buzz saw' excuse."

"Not only did I not get compensated for my loss of limbs, but the government told me I need to get a new job as soon as possible."

"You still have legs, don't you?"

"Yes."

"There you bloody go, then. Use them to operate ya buzz saw and do a good job this time. Now, ring ya old employer up and apologise for being such a blowhard. They might take you back, despite all ya winging and whining. Next!"

Gorgonzola stepped up. "You've got to help me, Nelly! I can't find my underpants."

"Are ya teking the bloody piss?"

"Please, Nelly. This is urgent. I have to collect the World Peace Prize this evening."

"This is a wind up. They're on ya bloody head."

Gorgonzola scoffed. "I don't need your no nonsense insults! If you're not going to help me, I'm out of here!" Gorgonzola burst into tears and stormed out of the office.

Gorgonzola was desperate so he sended the Pied Piper a message a twitter.

@PiedPiper Help me find my underpants. #Sorrynotsorry #tbhcba #tbfattheendofthedaythough

The Pied Piper came, eating a meat and potato pie which included meat and potato. "What do you want sexy gorilla?"

"Mi el pants. They gone missing."

"Don't worry. I'll play my flute."

The Pied Piper burnt over and sucked himself off, playing a fantastical tune as he did. Everybody within a 2 million mile radius took their pants off and gave their underpants to the Pied Piper.

"Any of these yours, gorilla?"

Gorgonzola: "Forget it. I'll never find my them." **THE END**

Just kidding. WE GO AGAIN!

Mis Shobss was in the centre of the Mall of America, shouting the world's secrets at the braindead masses, for she knew the truth. Humans didn't rule the world…Sharks did. "Man didn't take the first step on the moon!" she shouted. Miss Shobss knew the truth. The first living thing to get to the moon was a shark. "It swam so deep into the ocean that it fell off the planet!" Meanwhile, Gorgonzola decided to enter UK number 1 hit show The Apprentice to try and get some money to find his underpants.

"What's your business idea?" Lord Buger asked him.

"Lord Buger, I would like for you to invest 2 million pounds in me, so I can find my underpants."

"I like it," said Lord Buger. "You remind me of me. You're on the show."

Week 1 — Lord Buger. "Your task today is to clean my bedroom. Whoever does the shitest job will be insulted in front of everybody, before being fired."

Generic candidate 1: "I clean bedrooms for a living. I should be project manager."

Gorgonzola: "I don't even have a bedroom, but I'm extremely passive aggressive and I shout loudly."

Generic candidate 2: "Oh, great point, Gorgonzola. You should be project manager!"

40 minutes later…

Lord Buger: "This is an absolute shambles! I asked you to clean my bedroom, and you spent the entire afternoon painting my neighbour's fence!"

Gorgonzola: "I agree, Lord Buger. In hindsight, that was probably a bad idea."

Karen: "You're a bit of a thick cunt, aren't you?"

Gorgonzola: "I put my hands up, Karen; I am a bit of a thick cunt."

Lord Buger: "Tell me, Gorgonzola, why should I allow you to stay in this process?"

Gorgonzola: "Lord Buger, I —"

Lord Buger: "I don't wanna hear anymore. Gorgonzola, you're a complete arsehole, and for that reason, you're fired."

Gorgonzola: "Thank you for firing me on national television, Lord Buger. It has been a wonderful experience."

A failed attempt to win The Apprentice, Gorgonzola would have to find his underpants another way.

Then Mum asked Smart-arse McYoghurtNeck, "Would you like some presents for Christmas?"

"No," said Smart-arse McYoghurtNeck. "I would like some futures."

Smeanwhile, Gorgonzola was in the last two of this week's X-Factor.

Simon Bowell Problems: "I'm afraid we've come to a split decision. Which means we're going to have to take the vote to apartheid."

Shmeanwhile, it was bellybutton Monday at the local elementary school, and the dinner ladies were serving fluff from their own bellybuttons to the children.

Meanwhile, Billy Crevis has a meeting with his agent…

Agent: This is absolutely terrible. Are you trying to write the first story of the going off on a tangent era?

Billy: I was trying to be unique.

Agent: There's new unique, and then there is just bad. If you're gonna be bad, at least take inspiration from something bad that makes sense. Here.

Billy: How to Polish a Turd? What is this?

Agent: That's the book you're going to take inspiration from. The writer seems to have the same intelligence levels as you. Just don't make it too obvious you're ripping it off.

How 2 Pollinate a Turd

Buy Billy Crevis

About da Author

Billy Crevis wrote his 827th novel How to Abolish a Nerd during security checks at the airport.

2 U

Warning: The following story has not been edited, though let's be honest, grammar dont matter as long as you know what I'm on abowt. On the offhand that ur a real jobsworth about that type of thing, I have included an erotic pictures in hope that you let things slide. Thank me when ur enjoying yourself tonight:

(.)(.)

And 4 you ladies, I have included this throbbing beauty (my own might I add). Just make sure your parents don't catch you looking:

8-----------------------D

Kurly da Klown did a shit in the till. 'Quick!' he shouted. 'Colonel Sanders is coming. Poo on everything!' Rodney pulled his pants down and heaved. 'Hurry!' Kurly screamed.

'I can't,' Rodney cried. 'I glued my bum hole shut.'

Just then, Colonel Sanders entered Burger Flaps. Kurly gulped. 'Colonel. I wasn't expecting you.'

'Oh, you don't know how right you are.' The Colonel beamed a big grin. 'You were expecting Colonel Sanders. There's only one colonel in this room, and he don't fuck no chickens.' Colonel Sanders pulled his face off to reveal...

'OH MY!' Michael Cole shouted. 'That's ... That's Colonel Gadafi! What's he doing here?'

'Ha-ha! I was working for KFD all along!' Gadafi pulled out a family bucket. 'Kentucky Fried dogs, bitches!'

Gadafi fell into a black hole.

A woman with a furry growler came up 2 the counter. The woman snorted. 'I'm a hipster and I'm like to try new things. I'm trying to eat this burger using my vagina but your fries have clogged it shut.' Appropriately, she sounded like a woman who shoved cocktail sausages up her nose.

'Don't worry,' Rodney said. 'I am a plumber. I will unclog your vagina.' Rednoy didn't think the woman deserved to have her vagina unclogged and had a plan. A huge grin spread across his face. He knew how to get out of this.

'Mr Klown,' he said, smiling with joy at his genius idea. 'I'm afraid I must go home. I am feeling terrbily ill,' he laughed.

Kurly gasped. 'Oh dear. What's the problem?'

'There is a bat flying around my mouth and I cannot get it out.' XD <- Rednoy's face. 'It keeps giving me ulcers.' Rednoy's willy -> 8----D

'Oh deary me,' said Kurly. 'Before you go, let me give you something for good luck.' Kurly took Rodney by the hand and gazed into his eyes. He pressed his thick red lips against Rodney's and stuck his tongue down his throat. 'Does that feel better sugar?'

Rodney did a roly-poly. 'You had me at herro.'

Rodney went to da carpark where his pet tiger was parked. His tiger wore a jetpack and had an 11-inch willy. 'Tough day at the office kid?' Mr Tiger asked.

Rodney turned his frown upside down. 'Let's go jack off.'

Mr Tiger winked at him. 'That's the spirit kid.' Rodney jumped on his back, and Mr Tiger set off on his jetpack.

Rodney grunted when he got home. His living room was full of his girlfriend's mates pooing in each other's mouths. He saw Bridget on the phone. His eyes set ablaze. 'What the hell are you doing?'

'I'm voting for Nigeria to win Eurovision. Do you have a problem wid dat?'

'Nigeria? Ni-god-damn-fucking-geria? They're not even in Europe anymore. They moved the country to Russia, remember?'

'Too late! I've already voted for Brexit to win.'

'Why'd you do that you dumb broad? I was saving our money so we could vote on the x-factor final!'

Suddenly, Boobs McBoobies speared the door down. Boobs McBobblehat was Rednoy's next house neighbour and he had a pair of breasts on his head. 'Will you lot pipe down? I'm trying to do the bleep test. I can't hear the bleep coz of your annoying voices.'

'You're doing the bleep test eh? Try outrun this!' Rodney picked up the lawnmower and whacked Boobs McBrocolli's breasts. 'How d'ya like them apples?'

Tits McTadpole screamed. 'That's it radish head. You gon die now.' Bridget put Rodney in the bath and pulled the plug. He went down the drain and drowned.

Rodney awoke on Noah's Arc. It was jam-packed full with giraffes. 'What happened?' Rodney asked. 'Where r the rest of the animals?'

'We Giraffe's iz sick of being overlooked,' said Gertrude da G-raf. 'There int 1 gud g-raf eva. Name 1.'

Rodney shrugged. 'Shrek 2 was a good film.'

'That don't count!' Gertrude snapped. 'We aint gon take it no more. We are hijacking this ark until we iz declared da best.'

Kamila the camel came floating on the sea. 'One foot in front of the othr!' she yelled. 'That's how swimming is done!'

Gertrude puked. 'You think camel's iz better dan giraffes? Very well. We shall duel.' Gertrude began. 'We giraffe's iz so tall we suffer from excruciating neck pain. That's why giraffe's iz da best.'

Kamila responded. 'Oh yeah? Well us camels have to carry these motherfucking humps on our back, which not only break us down but also make us look like a bunch of stupid arseholes. That's why camels iz da best.'

'Oh yeah? We giraffe's iz so pathetic that if one of us got the sniffles we'd all be extinct by sundown. That's why giraffe's iz da best.'

'Oh yeah? Well us camels are such pussies that we refuse to eat our sandwiches outside, just in case the dinner lady tells us off for getting crumbs on the desert. That's why camelz iz da best.'

'Lads!' shouted Rodney. 'There's only one way to settle this. Hoops.' Rodney pulled his pants down. 'the first one to throw a donut over my erect willy wins.' Kamila and Gertrude had to be very accurate. Rodney's willy was only 1.33333 decibels recurring.

Gertrude threw her donut. She thought she had won. 'Yes! I threw the donut over your tinkler.'

'Sorry Gertrude,' said Rodney. 'You threw the donut over my left willy. The game was to throw the donut over my right willy.'

Kamila smiled. 'My time to shine.' She raised her paw. 'Hokus Pokus.' The hula hoop fit snugly onto Rodney's willy.

'What the fuck?' Getrude shouted. 'You cheated you bum sniffer. You can't use magic.'

'WOT YA ON ABOWT? I DINT EVEN DO OWT!'

'Fine, have it your way. Magic it is. I hope you're happy for interfering Rodney. I sentence you to a foreign world! Alakazam!'

POOF! and Rodney were gone.

The Graham Norton Show

Welcum to the Graham Norton's Finance show! With me your host, Noel Edmonds. My guest today is the author of the new greatest book of all time, How to Get Pooed On. Ladies and Gentlemen, Billy Cunt-Nuts!

WOOOOOOOOOOOOOOOOOOOOOOOOOO!

It's a pleasure to have you here Misses Cunt-Nuts.

It's a pleasure to be here Desmond Tutu.

Before we go have sex backstage, tell me, what are all the hidden meanings and secrets in your story?

That's a sexy question, Desmond. Chapter 1 is about how democracy. Chapter 2 is about the Ozone lair. Chapter 3 is...

Yawn! Wow Misses Cunt-Nuts. You're putting us all to sleep with that fucking boring story!

HAHAHAHAHAHAHAHAHAHAHAHAHAHAHAHAHAHAHAHA!

We might as well get my next guest out since you're such a blowhard. Don't go anywhere, because coming up after the break, the world's biggest jew face, Watto, will be on the sofa!

Rodney found himself somewhere in the southern half of England, which if he looked at on a map wouldn't have given him a clear destination, since every place in the south was represented by an orc getting bummed up the arse by Sergeant Bash.

He found himself sat next to a girl called Zara, who was the spitting image of Waluigi. Rodney cried the rain that fills the river temz. 'Am so sad. Am homesick.'

Zara put an arm around him. 'Whenever I'm sad, I think of my favourite story. I will tell it to you. The teacher asks the student 'What do you want to be when you're older?' The student says 'I want to be a landowner so I can kick poor families off my land so they become homeless.' The teacher says 'You don't understand the question'. The student says 'You don't understand life.''

Rednoy smiley-wiley's. 'You know, me and you aren't so different. We have the same ambitions. I've started exercising three times a month to get that perfect body. We are the ones who push ourselves.'

'I admire you for wanting to lose weight. I'd give swimming a crack if I were u. Drink two cups of chlorine water a day and you'll be well in shape.'

'Awesome. I'm trying to become hexagon shape. What do you use as a cup?'

'Johnstone's Paint Trophy. U?'

'Toilet roll.'

'True dat. Toilet rolls are a great choice of cup.'

Rodney looked around at her surroundings. 'How serious is the threat in this world?'

'Pretty serious,' said Zara. 'Henry Ford has entrapped the world in a giant washing machine. Now Robert Mugabe won't be able to get back in when he returns from his holiday on the moon. We must open the washing machine door before Mugabe gets angry and uses his helium arms to push the Earth in the sun.'

'Wowza. We better get to work.'

'Sorry Rodney. I must go. Tonight is my grandma's piano recital. I couldn't possibly miss it. A friend you're familiar with will guide you inspread.'

Duncan jumped out of Rodney's bowl of coco pops. 'Hi Duncan!' said Duncan.

'Hi Duncan!' said Rodney

Duncan was Rodney's best friend. He had an 8-inch willy when soft and a 4-inch willy when hard. Duncan liked to stand at bus stops, then run away when a bus stopped. 'Come on Rodney,' said Duncan. 'We must become university students so we can learn how to open a washing machine door.'

Ducan + Rodknee entered the lecture hall via teleprompter. Their new university teacher was Mr Crabbs. Mr Crabs owned the Crusty Crabb and was the lead singer of ACDC.

All of a sundden, Rodney suddenly noticed that everybody in the lecture hall was black. He was terrified they would misinterpret anything he said as racist. He had to make them think he was black. His only hope was to somehow make them all think he was No 1 black rapper, Michael Buble.

The tension was too much for Rodney. He had to say something to be sure they were off his case. He stood up and risked it all. He freestyled. 'I come from Spain, my mum's called Dwayne. I eat using my mouth, my favourite pole is south. Word dawg.' He sat back down. Now was the moment of truth. Had they fallen for it?

The first black person spoke. 'Is that Clare Balding?'

Rodney's heart dropped. Had he accidently convinced them he was Clare Balding? If he had, it marked the end of Bel Tine forever.

'No,' said a much more authoritative black persona. 'That's not Clare Balding at all.' Rodney gulped in anticipation of the black man's next words. 'I know who that is.' ... 'That's none other than No 1 hit rapper, Michael Buble!'

Rednoy's plan had worked. He had fooled them all and now he was one of them. Where The Hood At? hit over the tannoy and everybody got up and danced. Rodney was allowed to stay.

Mr Kurbs handed out the end of lesson exam. Since there were too many students, all exams were done under sudden death rules. If you got a question wrong, you got kicked out of uni. Rodney opened to question 1.

1) What is the secret ingredient of the Crabee Patty?
    a. Treaty of Versailles
    b. Garden gnome
    c. Sun burnt

Rodney didn't know the answer so he gave up. Fortunately, it was a menstrual question, so by not answering he gave the correct answer. Round 2.

2) What would you like for your birthday? (question submitted by dad)
    a. Leveson Inquiry
    b. Dairylea Dunker
    c. Peg leg

Bognor Regis didn't know. He...

Time skip!

Rodney answered all the qweshchuns. Ant and Dec made their way onto the floor. 'HOWAY! BECAUSE YA CARECTLEE ANSAD ALL DA QUESTYANS, YA GET TO STAY AT UNEE! NOW YA CAN STICK WITH YA PRIZE, OR IF YA GAMBAL, YA CAN WIN DA FOLLAWIN.'

That's right Anton Dubec. If Rodney gambles,,,,, he can win an all exclusive trip to Guantanamo Bay!

'That doesn't sound very good,' said Rodney.

'HOWAY YA TWAT! ITS PRACTACLEE A FREE HOLADAY! WHAT DOES DA PUBLIC SAY?'

Gamble! Gamble!

'WHAT A YA SAY RODNEE?'

'Well, even though I'm a certified moron and I fluked my way through every question, I'm going to give into the peer pressure of all these people I will never see again and gamble.'

'HOWAY YA TWAT! E's GONNA GAMBAL!'

Okay, Rodney, you've decided to gamble! For a trip to Guantanamo Bay answer the following question. Are you ready?

'Yes.'

EHT-ERNT (That be the sound of a buzzer)! Incorrect. You are not ready for a vaxination to Guacamole Bay and you never will be. You are hereby banished from uni 4ever

And so Duncan and Wodney had been Kicked out of uni. If only they could find a door, they could get back in. 'Look!' said Duncan. He pointed to a group of people lined up in a line, each person holding onto the back of the person standing in front of them. 'That conga might lead us back to uni.'

'R u sure?'

'I don't have a fucking clue, but for some unfathomable reason, it's our only chance.'

Duncan and Rodney joined the conga. Rodney wasn't quite sure how congas worked but thought everybody might make fun of him if he asked, so he kept silent. He followed his instincts, pulled down the pants of the man in front of him and put his fingers up his bum. The man looked like he was gonna turn around, but no, too late, da conga already started and so did the singing.

Come and do the conga

Make your willy longer

Na-na-na-na—hey!

Na-na-na-na—hey!

Come and do the conga

Make your willy longer

Na-na-na-na—hey!

Na-na-na-na—hey!

Unfortunately, the conga only led them into Shawna's Satnav Shop. Not too bad. At least they could buy a satnav. 'Ello,' said Shawna. 'It be me, Shawna. HOw can I help.' Shawna liked to go into public toilets and wipe her bogies on the toilet paper, so the next time someone went in to do a poo they'd wipe their bumhole with her bogies.

'Can we buy a satnav that will lead us to uni?'

'You want to buy a satnav that will get you to uni, do you? Our A Level 3A model should do the trick. That'll be 9 grand a year and 20 odd grand of debt please.'

Rodney brought the satnav. They turned it on and put in their desired destination. The satnav took up the voice of Mr Blobby. 'Go to Leeds Bradford Airport. At terminal 2, take a flight to Razgrad Bulgaria.'

Rodney scratched his head. 'I don't know. Are you sure this thing is pointing us in the right direction?'

'Of course,' said Shawna. 'You don't expect something so high in interest to be flawed do you?'

They didn't. They followed the satnav's instructions all the way to Varna airport, to Razgrad, where Mr Blobby sed 'Go to Varna Airport. At terminal 3, take a flight to Leeds Bradford airport.' They followed the instructions to Leeds Bradford airport. There, they followed the further instructions given until Mr Blobby sed 'You have reached your destination.' Rodney looked up. They were stood outside the entrance of Shawna's Satnav shop. They went inside.

'Hey!' Rodney shouted. 'Your satnav dint work. It only led us back here. Are you sure it works?'

'Golly gosh!' Shawna gasped. 'I have never known a satnav of mine not work. Where did you say you wanted to go?'

'Uni?'

'Ah, I know what it will be. For some reason, when you type in uni on that model of satnav, it automatically activates 'waste of time' mode. Here. Buy our B-tech Distinction model. That'll be 9 more grand a year thank you.'

Rodney paid the woman, sure the satnav would work this time. They put the satnav on and took to the road. Mr Blobby spoke, 'On the next road, turn right, then on the next road, turn right.' On the next road, they turned right, then on the road after, they turned right. Mr Blobby continued. 'On the next road, turn right.' They did. 'On the next road, turn right.' They did. 'On the next road, turn right, then on the next road, turn right.' It took Rodney and Duncan 3 years to realise they had been driving around in circles.

'Ah bollocks!' said Rodney. 'We've been done over.'

They went back to Shawna's satnav store. 'Hey!' Rodney shouted. 'Your satnav didn't work. It had us making right turns for about 3 years. Are you sure it works?'

'Golly gosh!' Shawna gasped – I'm basically copy and pasting the dialogue that took place a few lines up (Between Shawna saying 'Golly gosh!' and Rodney paying the woman). To save you from having to read the same thing again, let's jump forward to Shawna flogging them the next model of satnav. After 9 grand a year and all that...

They turned on the satnav and put in their destination. 'Take the next COAT WITH YOU TO SCHOOL, YOU DON'T WANT TO GET COLD.'

Rodney scratched his head. 'What?'

'In two miles turn THE TELE OFF BEFORE YOU GO OUT, STOP WASTING ELECTRICITY.' Rodney looked at the product they had bought. Turned out they'd actually bought a momnav. It continued to talk in the background. 'You are low on fuel. Stop at the next petrol station to fill up on LOW BUDGET POPCORN, 'COS I'M NOT BUYING YOU ANY OF THAT EXPENSIVE SHIT FROM THE CINEMA.'

'That's it!' Rodney shouted, throwing the momnav out of the car window. 'No more momnavs, or satnavs, or twatnavs or whatever the hell they're called. We're gonna have to find a way back into uni ourselves.'

Job Advert: Weatherman needed

Weatherman needed for tele.

Job Description: Required to guess what the weather is going to be like tomorrow—no need to worry, you don't have to be correct.

6

Apologies to anybody offended by anything in this book. No hate intended. Spread the love.

Flashback, Flashback, Flashback…

Henry Ford sat with his legs on the table in his Spaceship Mondeo. 'How's the washing machine coming along?' he asked assistant 1.

'Almost done, boss. Soon the world will have no way to buy automobiles from Japan.'

'Very good.' Henry Ford smiled. 'I guess you could say, *oil*'s well that ends well.' He winked. The assistants all groaned. They had been dealing with this shit from Henry Ford for way too long.

'We just need adjust the door,' said assistant 2.

'Soon it will all be in motion,' Henry Ford smiled. 'I guess you could say, the *wheel* is *wheel* in motion.' He winked.

The assistants all groaned. 'For fuck sake,' assistant 3 muttered under his breath.

'Mr Ford!' assistant 4 shouted. 'It's Kiichiro Toyoda! I think he's planning an attack!'

Henry Ford cocked his pistol. 'Get ready boys. It's time for a party.' Henry Ford smiled. 'I guess you could say, it's time *ford* a *fiesta*.' He winked.

'That's it!' assistant 5 shouted. 'I can't take it anymore!' He pulled the trigger of his gun and blew Henry Ford's head off.

The assistants were stunned. 'What did you do!' assistant 6 shouted.

'Somebody had to do it,' assistant 7 insisted. 'He was driving us all insane with his awful puns.'

'Never mind his awful puns,' assistant 8 shouted. 'who's gonna save us from the Japanese revolution now?'

All the odd numbered assistants raised their guns towards the even numbered assistants and vice versa.

'Gentlemen, gentlemen,' a new voice said. 'This isn't getting us anywhere.'

The assistants looked at the mysterious newcomer. It was him... The mysterious man in duck egg blue. 'Who the fucking hell are you?' assistant 9 asked.

'Why, I'm the man who's gonna take Ford into the stratosphere.'

Assistant $n+1$ said, 'You're going to help us defeat Kiichiro Toyoda?'

'Better yet,' said the mystery man. 'I'm gonna help us defeat the entire world. That washing machine you're building to surround Japan? You're going to disassemble it and build it around the entire Earth.'

'You want to surround the entire world?' said assistant $n+1$. 'There's not enough oil in the world to make a washing machine that big.'

The man in duck egg blue grinned. 'Oh, you really don't know my power, do you? First, let's deal with the Japanese.'

Rodney and Duncan joined a protest, in hope that would somehow lead them into getting back into uni. They didn't really know what the protesters were protesting for, but they liked to feel like they were part of big groups, so they joined in. They had a look around.

Just to be a hipster, I'm gonna name the following characters after Teletubbies (note: when you type in Teletubbies on Word, it's suggestion to make it a grammatically correct word is Timetables – WTF?). First, there was Tinky Winky. He was a right smelly bastard. Everybody called him Tinky Winky the stinky wanker. 'Pew-wee, Tinky Winky the stinky wanker,' Rodney said whilst clutching his nose. 'You smell like you've been dead for fifteen years.'

Tinky Winky: 'Rodney, I have been dead inside ever since Noo Noo died. Who else is gonna suck me off?'

Next was Dipsy. He was walking towards Rodney and Duncan when he fell down an exposed manhole he had not seen. 'Aw,' said Duncan. 'I always fancied the green one.'

Rodney shook his head. 'Anyone gonna tell us what we're rallying for?'

'I'll tell you,' said a man called Laa-Laa. 'We're rallying for abortion.'

'Alright. You mean for women who are pregnant and don't what to have a kid?'

'God no. We're rallying to force abortion upon people who've had it away too many times. We need to control the population somehow. In fact, here comes a subject now.'

Four men held scruff bag Sheila by her limbs as she struggled and spat at them. 'Hey, ya fucking dickedz! What da fuck are ya doing!'

'Scruffbag Sheila has had four different kids to four different men,' Milo explained. 'We wouldn't even mind that she hasn't had a job in twenty years if her oldest son didn't go around setting people's hair on fire.'

'How are you going to get her to have an abortion?' Rodney asked.

'Oh, don't worry. We're going to seal her vagina shut with cement.' So it was that Sheila and scruff bags everywhere had their vaginas sealed shut by cement to save the population.

'Looks like you'll be having a lot of celebrities to round up,' said Rodney. 'They love to have as many kids as they can.'

'Don't be silly Rodney. Everybody knows overpopulation is a problem created by the poor.'

Meanwhile, Dipsy crawled back out of the manhole. 'Hey Dipsy,' said Po. 'Go jump off that cliff.'

'I don't know,' said Dipsy. 'I think I might splatter to death.'

'Of course not,' said Po. 'Have you never heard that saying? Pain is temporary, glory lasts forever.'

Dipsy cheered. 'Well, when you put it that way.'

He jumped off the cliff, and his head went flying off after it smacked against a rock. Two minutes later, a professional cliff diver died of the same cause. His mother smiled as she looked down at the sea. 'At least he died doing what he loved; trying to commit suicide.'

The doors of people pollution closing, the world's population had been saved... Wait a minute. I'm fading away. Where am I?

'Ah, look at me, God, here in the clouds. Who'd have thought, that I, God, would be a vagina? Who'd have thought, that I, God, would talk as if I had to make an extensive description about everything? Oh no, here comes somebody through the clouds. Who has come to see I, God?'

'God, we are the men's right movement. My name is Adam. We can't tell you how sick we are to find out that God is a vagina.'

'Of course, I, God, am a vagina. What else would I be?'

'That's beside the point. We are here to complain about the blatant sexism against men that exists throughout Earth.'

'Go on then.'

'First of all, how come women are allowed to have boobs and we're not? They get to pour milk on their cereal, whereas we have to cover ours with cum. It's not fair. We want boobs.'

'Erm, okay then. What's next?'

'Second of all, how come you only allow women to get pregnant? They always get maternity leave, whilst us men, us discriminated minority race known as men, have to work. If I was a woman, I'd be trying for a kid all the time, then I wouldn't have to work.'

'You do know that babies come out of the vagina? If I were to allow men to get pregnant, you'd have to give birth out of your cock.'

'So?'

'So? Try to fathom a full newborn baby coming out of your cock. You're telling me you want to basically be able to piss out a person?'

'If it'll get me out of the office for several months, yes. Plus, we'll have an excuse for having a beer belly. We can lie and say we're pregnant.'

'Any more ridiculous requests?'

'Yeah. We want that thing where they all bleed once a month.'

'Why the hell do you want to have a period?'

'Because, we want an excuse to be able to wear Tampax pads. They look well comfy.'

'Any more requests before I, God, send you back to your girlfriends?'

'No.'

'Well I, God, am going to send you back to a reality where you are about to give birth. 3,2,1, gone. Now I will leave it ten minutes before looking at what Adam's life is like... It has been ten minutes, let I, God, look.'

'Ow Eve, it hurts. It's like taking the world's biggest dump whilst constipated.'

'Honestly Adam, I don't know why you asked for the ability to get pregnant. You cry when a football hits you in the nuts. Now go make us a sandwich, love.'

'Of course honey.'

Billy waited in his cell at the police station – hang on, why am I in jail?

Mr Crevis, I am PC Nancy.

Police cuntstable Nancy?

Politically correct Nancy. I have several complaints about your story. You must amend your work before it may be published. Several Camels have rung in to complain that you have portrayed them all as pussies in chapter 2. In fact, one's on the phone for you now.

Oh, don't put him on the line – oh 4 Christ sake.

"Ere m8. Ya wanna mek all us camels look like pussies do ya? You wanna tek da mick about the mother fucking humps on us back? Why don't you come to da Gobi Desert m8 and say it to us face?'

Now, sir, I apologise –

'Of course ur apologise, ya pussy. Ya all talk and no walk ya pussy. I swear down, if ya run ya mouth again... I swear on mi mum... I'll fucking bear bang ya.'

Looks like you've learned your lesson, Mr Crevis. Now, why don't you go ahead and rewrite chapter 2.

Chapter 2 revisited

Gertrude puked. 'You think camel's iz better dan giraffe's? Very well. We shall duel.' Gertrude began. 'We giraffe's iz so tall we suffer from excruciating neck pain. That's why giraffe's iz da best.'

Kamila responded. 'Oh yeah? Well us camels don't even have to carry these humps on our back, we only do it cos we're well strong. I'll beat ur fucking dad up. That's why camels iz da best.'

'Oh yeah? We giraffe's iz so pathetic that if one of us got the sniffles we'd all be extinct by sundown. That's why giraffe's iz da best.'

'Oh yeah? Well us camels are so ard we take an annual trip to the south pole just for the bantz. That's why camelz iz da best.' Then Kamila blinked and killed Gertrude.

Eleven

Tara had a plan. She took the group to her friend Alec Cliché's house. His mother, Gail Cliché, answered the door. 'I'm all ears.'

'Is Alec in?'

'Of course, you can see the apple of my eye. Break a leg. Don't hold your breath, though, 'cause he might get cold feet when he hears the cavalry coming. Touch wood he doesn't get ants in his pants and make a mountain out of a molehill.'

They went up to Alec's room via the living room, which Tara noticed had once again been decorated. As well as being a cliché dispenser, Alec's mum was one of those people who was never satisfied with what her house looked like. It was a good job she wasn't in charge of decorating the universe. 'The moon's all right—a bit knackered, though, innit? Take it down and put a leather one up.'

Alec's bedroom: Lair to the man who entered Internet forums with a mouse of fire. 'Alec. These are my friends I told you about.' Tara touched Alec on the shoulder as she addressed him. His eyes never strayed from the double screen.

'One minute,' Alec said. 'Got a few jobs to do.' And he did them all via command prompt. First, he went on Twitter and corrected the spelling mistakes of all the celebrities he didn't like—the only people he followed for some reason.

@Sassycomedian: I didn't know you're cat liked to do the river dance.

@AlecBootyHunter69: @Sassycomedian You're cat liked to do the river dance? It's Your, you moron. As in, Your cat deserves to drown in a river. Numbnuts.

@QuirkyDurky: I should of done my nails pink for the ceremony.

@AlecBootyHunter69: @QuirkyDurky You should of done your nails pink for the ceremony? It's should have, you slut. As in, you should have killed yourself as soon as you were born.

Hard to believe there are people who read solely to grill those who make the slightest grammatical mistake rather then for enjoyment.

Imagine if you were a postman and someone had spread their arse against the other side of the letter box just as you were about to post. **52.**

He then went on Facebook because he felt the need to share his anger with a bunch of people he hadn't seen since high school. Alec had been courting a girl online for a month. She had finally grown annoyed at him asking for tit pics every two seconds and blocked him. He posted, 'Every girl in the world is vain and evil. All the bitches care about is looks. I'd treat a girl like a princess, but all they want is to be married to a nasty jerk who treats them like dirt. Us nice guys always finish last.' Then he laughed at a fat girl's new profile picture.

Rodney noticed from Alec's newsfeed that he was friends with Lavender Youth. She was clearly shitfaced in her profile picture, lying on the ground in a miniskirt with her legs up in the air and two pints in her hands. 'Lol! Rate good nyt wiv da besties! I got fooking munted XD,' her status said. At least Lavender's post was an accurate portrayal of the person she was in real life. Rodney could imagine she was the type of person who didn't consider it a good night out until her hair was drenched in someone else's puke, and she had been kicked out of a taxi for making an outrageous racist remark to the driver.

Rodney could never call anything Johnny posted genuine. Johnny was a keen poster of 'inspirational' quotes, despite never doing anything inspirational—still, he got forty-five likes, so he must have been doing something right. His latest post said, 'Nobody ever regretted not doing enough work in life.' This inspired Rodney to think the thought, 'Nobody ever regretted not posting enough inspirational quotes on Facebook, so stop doing it.' Lavender and Johnny weren't the only ones to post stuff on social media as if it were a lost art form. A general look at the posts on Facebook was a reminder that most people on the planet are secretly idiots—I should know because I am an idiot.

Lastly, Alec opened a music video of some band on YouTube and ranted in the comments section about how he didn't have to listen to some stupid advert to know about the song, how he was a real fan, and how their old stuff was much better. For ultimate condescension, he made sure to call everyone else in the comment section children.

After all that, Alec asked, 'What do you need me to do?'

'The Unlabelled King is a greedy liar who wants everybody to go to war with each other,' Tara said. 'I need you to spread a message online to everybody. Maybe you can hack into his system and get some dirt on him.'

'System.' Alec laughed. 'What a noob.' He cracked his fingers and got to work. He typed at a million words per second on the keyboard. In fact, he didn't even type. He smashed his fist on the keyboard. In fact, he was so good at hacking that he head-butted the keyboard with his face, and he still worked wonders on screen.

He used all the usual hacker lingo. 'I just need to triangulate the binary code.' A waterfall of numbers came on screen. He successfully typed in the four-digit code because everybody knows that is how hacking works. 'Bingo!' he shouted, as is customary to say when hacking.

Tara couldn't contain her joy. 'You've gotten into his computer?'

'Highly unlikely,' Phoenix said. 'The man doesn't own a computer.'

'Never mind his computer,' Alec said. 'I've hacked into his dinner plates. We'll record a message so that next time he eats his dinner, he spits it all over himself in shock!'

'Just find info on him, thanks,' Tara said.

'I've hacked into his bottle of Mr Sheen. I can tell you how dirty his tabletops are.'

'Just useful info, thanks.'

'Okay, just useful info, then.'

Alec quickly scanned through the Unlabelled King's files that were saved on his bottle (can?) of Mr Sheen. Tara gasped. Something caught her attention. 'Go back to that.'

Everyone gasped when they inspected the picture closely. The reason the King wore the ridiculous overgrown sock on his head became apparent. He had a big floppy willy on his head.

Alec cracked his fingers. 'Time for this to go viral. I'll just sneak past the proxy and steal the algorithms, so I can hack into the modem and steal the…what's the word?'

'Bullshit?'

'Yeah, that's the one. I need to bullshit the bullshit, so I can perform the bullshit.'

Alec successfully did what he had to do. He sent the image across the web for the entire world to see. King Dickhead was soon trending.

Twelve

Rodney was on edge. He couldn't believe God hadn't called him to rest after yesterday's work. Tara's celebrations had made it seem like they had overthrown the Unlabelled King, yet here Rodney sat, in a restaurant with Johnny.

The waiter came over. 'Are you ready to order?' Rodney ordered a rare steak. Always one to outdo others, especially when it came to portraying stereotypical manliness, Johnny ordered his steak raw. Never mind if he got food poisoning, it would be worth it for the ego boost.

The lumbering oaf at the table next to them was keen to join the game. 'How would you like your steak done?' the waiter asked him.

'ALIVE.'

Johnny did a double-take. His face turned green when the waiter instantaneously brought out an alive cow for the oaf to eat. The oaf even had the audacity to wink at Johnny, despite the cow barging him and the table over.

'Can I get you any drinks?' the waiter asked.

'I'll have a pint of Stella,' said Rodney.

Johnny looked at the oaf, who would have been wearing a grin if not for the mooing cow's head sticking out of his mouth. Johnny grinned at his rival; he knew he could beat him. 'I'll have a pint of absinthe, please.' He smirked at the oaf.

The oaf spat the cow out and said, 'I'll have a real man's drink, please.'

'And what would that be?' said the waiter.

'*A pint of anti-freeze.*' The oaf's canines beamed with proudness at the delight of his manly request. Johnny lowered his head and turned back around in defeat.

A waiter soon came with the food and plonked it down in front of them. Rodney asked the waiter if he could have a steak knife like the one Johnny had been given. There was something off about the waiter Rodney couldn't put his finger on.

Nice foreshadowing, jerk! Way to give away the plot!

Nevertheless, the waiter said he would get him a steak knife. Rodney and Johnny talked. 'I'm lost, Johnny. We just exposed the Unlabelled King as literally the world's most powerful dickhead. Why hasn't there been public uproar?'

'Little did we know, there's a difference between a man who is a dickhead and a man who actually has a dick on his head. Our plan has only increased his popularity. The people are calling him brave and iconic for overcoming such an evolutionary misfortune. The hackers are the ones being called cowards.'

'But all I've heard in here tonight is people laughing at the man's head and how weird it is.'

'That's the way people are. They'll laugh at him in their private groups, but condemn anyone who does it on a grand scale.'

'What do you suppose we do? I'm desperate to be dead.'

'Tara's bought us some disguises. We're going back to uni to see if we can find any more information. There's a poetry workshop tomorrow, so I imagine there'll be plenty of informants there.' Johnny stood up, wiping his mouth with his napkin. 'It has been my pleasure eating Rodney. I'll see you tomorrow. This commotion has caused a tremendous sweat on my face. I need a shave.'

'You don't even have a beard.'

'Skin's a beard, bro. Gotta get air to that skull.' Johnny left Rod—hang on a minute, he's already leaving? He had three chips, for Christ's sake. Granted, his steak was raw, but he didn't even eat any of his sides. What the hell was the point in going to a restaurant when all he needed to do was exchange dialogue? Why not do it over the phone and save the unnecessary unrealism of the scene? Oi! Johnny! I'm talking to you. Come back and finish your meal. Oh, he's already gone. Deary me.

The waiter plonked a steak knife and a handful of Yorkshire puddings on Rodney's plate. 'For your troubles, sir.'

Rodney raised an eyebrow. 'Will these be added to my bill?'

'They are on the house, sir.' The waiter walked away.

Rodney's white-rose sense was tingling. No sane man gave away Yorkshire puddings for free.

Out on the streets, a call from an alleyway caught Johnny off guard. 'Oi! Look and suck for only thirty pounds!' He jumped when he recognised Alec in full makeup, a miniskirt, and a gag in his mouth. He jumped once more when he realised who had shouted. A woman stood behind Alec, holding him by a chain. For some reason, Officer Nancy was wearing a massive feathered cap and a long fur coat.

'Officer Nancy? What are you doing?'

'I'm giving this little hoodlum what he deserves for stealing private information from the King. The law clearly states that hackers are to be prostituted.'

'Are you sure it doesn't state that they're meant to be prosecuted?'

'Did you go to the police academy, Johnny?'

'No.'

'Then excuse me if I don't listen to your opinion. I arrest bad guys for a living. I think I know what the law says. I ought to have you arrested for fraud. Anyway, this guy says somebody else put him up to the hacking. If you have any ideas, you'll ring 666 won't you?'

'You mean 999?'

'No, Johnny, not the number of the devil. I mean the police services, you idiot. You'll ring if you know owt, won't you?'

Johnny looked at Alec, who was desperately trying to fight the gag in his mouth to dob him in it. 'Sure. Of course I will.'

'Good stuff, Johnny. By the way, you don't know anywhere to drop prostitutes off, do you? Are there not any playgroups they can go to?'

'Sorry Nancy, I don't think they do day cares for prostitutes. Have you tried offloading him in the skip?'

'Might do. It's just that I thought there were houses that a load of them hung out in? Never mind. I'll probably just put him in the bin, like you said. I have to go, you see. A toddler's been spotted walking around ASDA eating a packet of Walkers before they've been paid for. He'll be chained to a trolley by the time I get there.'

Meanwhile, Rodney dug his fork into the Yorkshire pudding and took a bite. As the food hit his stomach, the thought hit his head.

BOOM!

He knew there was something fishy about those Yorkshire puddings.

Thirteen

Rodney awoke in a land of fire and brimstone, where a giant pair of testicles loomed over him. It wasn't the heat that made his blood boil. 'I am truly dead this time? I thought you said there was no afterlife?'

'I'm God, Rodney. I say a lot of things. I could say Jesus fed five thousand people with two fish, and they wouldn't question it. Anyway, Rod, I'll be honest; Hell didn't exist the first time you found yourself at my feet—or balls. I decided to listen to the prayers people send me for once and discovered they are all absolutely terrified of doing anything to peeve me off because they think I'll punish them. Then I had a light-bulb moment. I can make anybody do whatever I want by threatening to send them to Hell if they don't do as I say. So here it is, Rodney. I have created Hell. What do you think?'

'Meh. Bit warm. Nowt too unbearable. You might want to turn the heating up a bit. What do you plan on doing here to make people suffer?'

'Oh-ho-ho, I have created a torturous schedule to put people through their paces, Rodney. First, the sinners will be incinerated and kicked between the legs for nine hours in a row. Then, a million annoying voices will scream in their head for eight hours. Finally, the sinners will have a few hours to regenerate before the process takes place all over again. What do you think of that?'

'So basically if you're bad and you die, you go to a slightly hotter version of Earth?'

'I suppose you do. Either way, you don't want to end up here, do you?'

'No, I do not. I would like that eternal rest you promised me.'

'Good. Let the possible existence of Hell motivate you to do things you don't want to do. Right now on alternative Earth, you are under the rubble of the blown-up restaurant. Nobody knows that it was the tainted Yorkshire pudding that caused the place to explode, so when you are found, I have made it so you will still be in one piece. You were caught off guard by a worker of the Unlabelled King. Let this be a lesson to you to keep your eyes peeled. You forget that I am God and that my rationality is all over the shop. Next time you die, I might not be kind enough to send you back. As for now, are you ready to go back?'

'Suppose so. The sooner I get this ridiculous problem solved, the better.'

God sent Rodney back to life. He was pulled out of the rubble by a fireman and was soon walking around at his own free will again.

Fourteen

Rodney and Johnny entered the library in their disguises. Rodney wore a pair of overalls made out of lemon skin, while Johnny wore nothing but a sock on his nob. Johnny was overwhelmed by the sheer number of books stacked upon the shelves. 'Wow,' he said. 'Isn't it amazing how they make trees out of books?' He picked out a copy of the famous fable 'The Boy Who Cried Wolf: the literal version.'

Villager 1: 'For God's sake, don't make him cry! You don't want to know what will happen.'

Villager 2: 'What the hell! Why is a wolf pouring out of his eye? Argh! It's eating my legs!'

Meanwhile, in another room of the university, Trent Foot had volunteered to be an examiner and was doing his best to get the maths students disqualified. He tapped a student on the shoulder. '*Psst.*'

'What?'

'Ah! No talking in the exam! That's a fail!'

He flashed his phone in a girl's face. She looked up. 'Aha! The answers for question 2a are on this screen! Disqualified!'

Rodney and Johnny took their place in the poetry circle. A teacher called Dave Chatte taught the class because it is important to have French words in a book in order for it to be any good. He wore a shirt that had '*Vas te faire encule. Apprendre le français*' printed upon it.

Johnny read out 'Humpty Dumpty.' Here's a thought: Why are all the nursery rhymes about people having accidents? Humpty Dumpty fell off a wall, Jack fell down and broke his crown, and the old man went to bed and bumped his head. You can guarantee there wouldn't be a song about Humpty Dumpty if he'd have fallen today. He'd be getting compensated for being a clumsy oaf. 'Humpty Dumpty sat on the wall, Humpty Dumpty had a great fall, so he put in a claim against the unfortunate sods who owned the wall and won £10,000.' Never mind Alexandr the meerkat; you can all thank me when Injury Lawyers 4 U have an endless amount of annoying adverts featuring Humpty Dumpty suing people.

A smug-looking chap called Timothy Benedict stood up and said, 'If I may read my own poem. I call it…'Atonement's Chardonnay."' He continued:

Do thou lie in fields of yonder
Or do thou cry in bowls of ambiguity
Mine river is sentimental yet surrendered
A fragment of porcelain seals my charade

Rodney looked around the room. He could not believe the awe expressed on everyone's face for the complete nonsense coming out of Benedict's mouth.

Let us yield to hampers of neuroethology
And let thine harpoon the blunder

'Thine!' a student shouted, punching the air in triumph. 'Thine! He said thine! Slobber all over my nuts! He said thine! That is genius!'

The poem continued until it concluded—so it might have been just as well to say that the poem concluded. Benedict received a round of applause. 'I've never heard such dribble in my life,' Rodney moaned.

Benedict snarled. 'I'd expect no other opinion from an uneducated fool. I bet you can't even read idioglossia.'

'Ha! Idioglossia!' Mr Chatte bellowed. 'What a conformist. I only read hieroglyphs.'

Suddenly, Rodney unlocked the special ability of artificial profoundness, and in that moment, he could find deep meaning in Benedict's twaddle. A foreign voice submerged his internal monologue. '*Do thou lie in fields of yonder? Or do thou cry in bowls of ambiguity? By Jove, I've got it!*'

Who are you? Rodney asked the new voice inside his head. It ignored him and continued to find meaning in Benedict's twaddle.

'*It all makes sense! Do thou lie in fields of yonder; do you live in the land of your fantasies? Do thou cry in bowls of ambiguity; are you torn by a life of direction that is unclear?*'

I don't see how this helps me in any way.

'*Mine river is sentimental yet surrendered; he has long accepted the romances of his have died. A fragment of porcelain seals my charade; he wears his materialistic items to hide his true personality. Yes! That is it! There is something hidden about the poser king you must find to dethrone him.*'

Go on...

'Let us yield to hampers of neuroethology and let thine harpoon the blunder;
he must store his tears in order to rid himself of the pain they cause him. It is
clear now. Something has happened to the poser king in the past to make him the
way he is. There lies a giant well in the middle of Oldham. It is said that all of
the world's secrets lie at the bottom. Go there, and you may see what weaknesses
the poser king has.'

All that information from a senseless poem, Rodney thought. Perhaps,
there is reason to believe you can find meaning in anything.
Meaningful or not, he was one step closer to ending this moronic
tale. He would make sure to tell the others what he had found out.
The glorious town of Oldham awaited them. (In case you couldn't
detect the sarcasm in that last sentence, I strongly advise you never to
visit Oldham—ever.)

Meanwhile, in Italy...

Fifteen

General Speroni, a man who looked like he'd witnessed the Ice Age, was in the middle of a meeting with the Italian Supreme Defence Council when Luciano yanked the door open. 'General Speroni, I have urgent news for you,' he for some reason said in English.

'Please, one second.' The General followed Luciano outside of the office. 'What the fuck is this?' Speroni shouted, unaware his associates in the meeting could clearly hear his voice.

'Sir, there is absolute chaos in Naples.'

Speroni growled. 'I refuse to believe for one second there is a place called Nipples.'

'Not Nipples, sir. Naples.'

'Even so, I know you're lying. There is no such place as Naples. Don't you know I learned geography in America? Everybody knows Rome and Milan are the only two cities in Italy.'

'I swear Naples exists, sir. Look.' Luciano pulled out a globe he had hidden up his butt. 'See here. Naples.' He pointed.

Speroni gasped. 'What do you know. There are more than two places in Italy. Who'd have thought, America ignorant to other cultures? This must be a first,' said the leader of whatever the hell the Italian version of the army is called—who cares? 'What is the problem in this here Nipples?'

'Naples, sir. Come with me. I'll show you.'

A member of the meeting popped his head out of the office door. 'Is this going to take much longer?'

'The meeting is over,' Speroni said. 'You may go home.'

'I hate to break it to you, but we still have not found a solution to the smegma pandemic—'

'Shut the hell up and go home!' Speroni shouted. An annoyed group of Italians exited the office, doing that thing with their hands all Italians do when they're angry.

Luciano led Speroni down a hallway to a room that contained a giant computer screen. A woman wearing a headset greeted him. 'General, thank Luciano Pavarotti you are here! My name is Christie.' Speroni smiled as he cupped her hands in his. 'Rest assured, my lady, once I have saved the world, I will come back here, and I will bone you.' Christie's smile fell off her face. 'So then, what appears to be the problem?'

'Well, sir, our agency in Naples have sent us these images, of what I cannot describe,' said a man called Simone, who had spaghetti for hair because Italy and all that.

The Italians looked at the computer screen. They watched ravaging human-sized sperm rip people's faces open with bottles of WKD. A pack of explosive Rizla hit the camera, causing the screen to fuzz. The Italian intelligence crew looked at Speroni for his reaction. 'Holy shit.'

'We have never seen creatures so vile. We have absolutely no idea what those things are. I could try to do some tests,' Christie suggested.

A light bulb pinged in Speroni's head. 'I have a better idea. You there, what is your name again?'

'It's Luciano, sir.'

'Luciano, get me a phone. I need to make a call to President Lippi.' Luciano handed the General his phone. A few digits later, Speroni was in contact with President Roberto Lippi.

'Hello.'

'Mr President.'

'Who is this?'

'Why, it's the General, of course.'

'Ah, Gianluca! Have you recovered from your birthday bash?'

'My friend, there was so much *fica* around that night!'

'Tell me about it! I totally boned that blonde bitch! The one with the tattoo.'

'No way! I did her as well! Really nice *fica*, don't you think?'

'Like driving a Ferrari through the front door of the Florence Cathedral!' Speroni continued laughing until he noticed Christie, Simone, Luciano, and the ghost of Pope Benedict glaring at him. 'Anyway, my friend, there are serious matters we must discuss.'

'Come on, Gianluca! We don't do serious matters. I'm shit at my job. I'm just in this for the amount of *fica* I get, ah!'

'Ha-ha! I hear you, Roberto!'

Christie snatched the phone out of Speroni's hands. 'The whole of Italy may be under threat!' she yelled down the line. 'These sticky creatures could potentially wipe out civilisation!'

'Wow, Gianluca! Who is this fiery little minx?'

Christie produced a comically large mallet and whacked the phone with it. Somehow, it didn't smash the phone, but went through it, coming out at the end of President Lippi's phone and smacking him on the head. The hit made a massive BADOING noise, and a big red bump grew out of Lippi's head, orbited by a halo of birds.

Luciano calmly took the phone from Christie and said, 'Sir, this is honestly the worst thing I have ever seen! So many people's lives are at risk!'

'Well, why didn't you say so!' Lippi shouted, causing Christie to groan. 'What is the exact problem?'

'I am sending the images to your phone now.'

'You have got to be shitting me!' Lippi bleeped down the line. 'My reputation will go down the shitter for this! I already have the press on my back for cleaning my plates with that Saudi prince's headdress. How was I supposed to know that wasn't a complementary dishcloth on his head?'

'Mr President, we are going to need a decision on what to do here.'

After no thought, Lippi said, 'General Speroni, round up the army. We are going to take these bastards by force.'

Simone jumped out of his seat. 'But you have seen those things! They will completely swallow our men!'

'We can't spit them away. We must penetrate them.'

Soon, the mutant sperm had devoured Napoli and had travelled to Bari. The afternoon sky was jet ~~black~~ African American. Naval fleets, Italian air force helicopters, and tanks arrived at the battered city, unaware if their weapons would do any damage to the disgusting threat. They lined up in front of the harbour. President Lippi, General Speroni, and Luciano stood alongside the soldiers and commanders.

'Why the hell am I here?' Luciano asked.

'We may need to examine these things for later,' Speroni replied. 'That is, if we kill them.'

'But I am not a scientist. I'm a secretary.'

'In Italy, they're basically the same thing.'

'But what about Christie? She seemed to know what she was talking about.'

Lippi trembled at the name. 'Of course not,' he said nervously. 'I'm sure you'll do a great job.'

Civilians hid inside buildings in a last attempt to avoid the sticky swimmers on the way. General Speroni wandered over to a woman who sat sobbing in front of a dead man's corpse. She embraced her distraught son in her arms. Speroni placed a tender hand on the child's back. 'Your father may be dead, my son, but I would still bone your mother.' The mother and son burst out crying. Speroni walked away. 'What's his problem?' he muttered under his breath. 'I only complimented his mother. Bastard.'

An army official, Oscar Carboni, shouted to the General. 'Sir, the unknowns are approaching.' The marching unborn closed in on the army. All cries stopped. Silence. The inbred, profane, obnoxious cum driblets from England were on their way (I'll let you decide which region of England that is a metaphor for *cough* Grimsby *cough*). 'Sir, on your command we will attack.' The General waited a very long five seconds. Silence ended. The squirms and snarls of Helly Hansen's angels had arrived.

BANG!

'Attack!' Speroni ordered. The battle to save Bari, and probably the whole of Italy, began. At first, the Italians actually tried to reason with the sperm, which any man with common sense knows is just stupid. The army grew terrified of the sperms' resistance to persuasion, so instead they announced it was happy hour and lunchtime karaoke at the White Horse, and they were all well happy. Most buggered off back to England.

Other sperm cells weren't so easily defeated. Speroni pondered to himself. *What kills sperm? Wait!* 'I know what to do! Pour Dr Pepper on them!' The Italians roared in sudden realisation of Speroni's genius. Dr Pepper! What a brilliant shout! Any boy between the ages eleven to fourteen knew not to drink the stuff, because it killed sperm. The Italians got a massive load of Dr Pepper and sprayed it everywhere.

Dr Pepper doesn't actually kill sperm. Putting your balls in the oven will.

'Aha! Yes! Run away, you cowards!' Lippi shouted. A monster—clearly a more advanced one, as it wore big loopy earrings—darted at him. The President's cries of *Aha!* soon changed to *Argh!* Fortunately for him, Speroni quickly pulled out a shotgun and blasted a hole through the monster's face. The monster flopped to the ground, and its sticky white blood splashed Lippi in the face.

'Phew,' Lippi sighed. 'I would not bone that crazy bitch…or would I?' The hordes of the unborn slowly retreated. The Italian army stood tall without any casualties. Italy had defeated the creatures with complete ease.

'Yes!' President Lippi cheered as he began the waves of celebration throughout Bari. This was a great victory for humanity that would forever go down in Italian history.

'I always knew we would kill those bastards! That is why I brought the celebration tank!' General Speroni announced. The entire Italian army roared in ecstasy.

'The celebration tank?' Luciano questioned. His confusion was answered when six naked ladies pulled up in a pink tank, unloaded several kegs of beer, and threw them out to the boisterous soldiers. Bari was on a high, and even Luciano joined in with the drunken celebrations.

BOOM!

'Err, what the hell was that?' Lippi asked, to no answer. The crowd stood in complete silence. A muffling umm echoed across Italy, and from the sky descended a colossal dildo. It would surely plough a hole through the entire country.

'Well, we're fucked—literally,' Lippi uttered.

Screams hijacked the city as the monstrous sex toy shadowed over Italy. Luciano scanned around. He saw something out of the corner of his eye and did a double take. General Speroni was running toward a helicopter. Luciano headed after him. 'General!' he cried. 'How are we going to stop that monster?'

'Well, I'm fucking off out of here,' Speroni replied as he started the helicopter.

'But, sir, that thing will take us all out.'

'Tell me again, young man, what is your name?'

'It's Luciano, sir.'

'Luciano, you are a stupid asshole! There is no way in hell we're stopping that thing, hence why I am doing a runner!'

President Lippi sprinted toward the helicopter. 'Wait!'

Speroni gave him the middle finger. 'Fuck you, Roberto! You stole my bitch!' He shut the helicopter doors and began to fly away. The President grabbed hold of the landing skids just as the helicopter ascended into the sky. He did not have the strength to hold on for very long and splattered to a quick instant death.

With the highest figures of authority now either dead or fleeing, it was up to Luciano, a man whose finest skill was taking minutes at meetings, to motivate the jaded army. He did what every leading actor in every movie involving a battle ever would do. He climbed atop the celebration tank.

'Men!' The confused soldiers turned toward Luciano. 'So is that thing going to kill us all? Now, it may be a two-hundred-foot-tall killer dildo, but we are Italy! We conquered Europe before, and we even helped end Jesus! Nothing can defeat us! We took down the filthy little sperms; now let's blow up that massive bell end! Because tonight, brothers and sisters, we take back something from someone!' The soldiers cheered for Luciano's heroic speech.

'Who the hell is that guy?' one solider whispered to another.

'I don't know, but he's shouting things in an enthusiastic way.'

'Oh yeah. Hooray! Down with the killer dildo!'

Soldiers started shooting at the giant dildo. 'Hey!' Carboni shouted to retrieve their attention. 'Now, obviously that thing is all the way up there, which means standing here and using your guns is pretty damn stupid. Your bullets will not reach.'

'We could wait for it to get closer,' suggested a soldier.

'Too risky. The way I see it, we are all going to have to fit inside the helicopters and fly toward the monster. There, we should be high enough and will have our strongest weapon in the choppers' torpedoes.'

'YEAHHHH!' shouted an Italian soldier who was wearing nothing but a jockstrap. 'LET'S DO THIS!' The Italians cheered in response.

'Yes, indeed! Men! Cram the choppers!' The soldiers followed Carboni's orders, including Luciano who squeezed into one of the vehicles. Thousands of soldiers crammed into helicopters only supposed to hold six people. Surprisingly, the Italians were incredibly optimistic they could defeat the massive dildo. Unsurprisingly, absolutely everyone either died from suffocation or from crashing into the ground when the helicopter engines failed.

The killer dildo plummeted through Italy and tore a gaping wound through the country. The whole of Italy collapsed as the dildo sank into the pits of the ocean. Ironically, the country shaped like a boot had been kicked off the face of the Earth.

Filler

I heard to be classed as a novel a story has to have at least forty thousand words, so I have included the following passages of nonsense to up my word count. Honestly, this chapter has as much point to it as the rest of the story. Here are some jokes.

Joke 1: 'Knock-knock.'

'Who's there?'

'The repo man. You've not been paying your council tax, so I'm here to take all your stuff.'

'The repo man, you've not been paying your council tax, so I'm here to take all your stuff who?'

'You can play dumb all you want, sir. It doesn't change the fact that come an hour's time, your house is going to be empty.'

Joke 2: 'Doctor, Doctor, I'm from the governing body of medical expertise. I'm here to shut you down for false medical advice.'

'I'll get my things.'

Joke 3: What do you call a man with no hair?

Bald.

Zara took Duncan and Rednoy to see her good friend Bubba. They let themselves in his house and sprant into his living room.

Bubba was watching the first Lord of the Rings. He shook his head as Isildur cut off Sauron's fingers. 'Why the hell didn't he just wear the ring on his cock? They wouldn't have been able to touch him under all that armour.'

'Bubba, it's me,' said Zara. 'We need your help.'

'No can do, love,' said Bubba. 'I'm planning on watching Babestation with little Bobby tonight. I'm gonna teach him how to whack one out.'

Rednoy smiled. 'Nothing like father-son time.'

'I know,' said Bubba. 'I can't believe I'm gonna teach my dad how to jack off.'

'Forget TV for a second will ya,' Zara said. 'We need you to get Rodney and Duncan back in uni. We came to you because we know you can write a bloody good TV complaint letter.'

'Alright. But let me watch the season finale of EastEnders first. I heard Pat does a poo on Peggy's chest.'

The finale of EastEnders was everything Bubba could have asked for. Ken Barlow even turned up and hit Phil Mitchell over the head with a corn on the cob. Bubba cracked his fingers. 'Now for serious matters.' He wrote the complaint letter, which I can't be arsed writing, so you're just gonna have to make something up in your head.

Progress Review

What do you think, sir?

'Bit linear in it? I wished you'd change the passage structure a bit.'

I put a flashback in there.

'Yeah, I'd like to see more changes. Hell, why not go a nonlinear route for writing dialogue? That would be different from the same passageways authors have been following forever.'

No, I meant the sound you make when you fart.

'At least something that's different is at least unique. Why would you want to be like everything else?'

Whatever man, I'll try your nonlinear approach if it gets you off my back.

'What does Donald Trump have to do with anything?'

Just because it's different doesn't mean it's any good.

'Ah, well of course you'd make a fart joke reference. That's all you ever do.'

Oh yeah, I agree you shouldn't just copy other people's work. But being unique could be anything. Why, you could have a bunch of characters who just speak in trump noises.

A Spanish man called El Ordenador came downstairs, wearing nothing but a pair of coconuts over his burger nips and a KitKat wrapper over his todger. 'I am ready he said.'

Mum gasped. 'You can't wear that she said. The Portuguese' will try to replace everyone's wallpaper with strips of donner meat if you do.

I don't care about the Portuguese 'shouted El Ordenador.' I want to be a pornstar.

'Mum gasped.' Don't say that in front of your dad. He wants you to pick people's noses for a living.

Just then 'Dad walked in. Good' morning 'El Ordenador.' Boy 'have I had a good day picking. Once you 'join the busin'ess I'll be able to move on to picking people's bums. That's where all the money is. I heard Un Sacapuntas' found 'the Midas up Moira's arsehole. A violent horrer came over Dad's face. You are wearing a suit made of of breadcrums he said 'sternly.'

'Dad' 'I don't' want to pick bogies for a living. 'I want to cum in people's mouths.'

Dads eyes bulged out of their sockets and EXPLODED! 'No sun of mein fuhrer is becoming a pawn star! You'll pick people's noses if I have to force u to do it!' Now, go back upstairs and put my dirty underpants on your head.

'NO! El Ordenador yelled as he cried upstairs. It was his life and he wouldn't have anybody dictate it. To cheer himself up, he rubbed shower gel in his eyes.

Just then, the TV turned itself on. 'BREAKING NEWS! Oil out spill drowns the entire country of Denmark. I repeat, the country Denmark is no more.' Ironically, the country called Denmark had been... Fuck that. It was Germany. Germany was no more. Ironically, the country called Germany had been germed off the face of the Earth.

Now that Ducan was gone, Rednoy had to go 2 uni alone. Today was book review day. It was Rodney's turn to review his book. 'For my book review, I chose to review The Very Hungry Caterpillar.'

'The Very Hungry Caterpillar?' asked a girl called Fellatio. 'What's that?'

'Don't talk shit Felicia,' said Mr Dildo. 'Everybody on the western hemisphere has heard of The Very Hungry Caterpillar. Get on with it Rodders.'

'Here is my review of The Hunger Cateripplar,' sed Rednoy. 'Although this book is based on a true story, it is obviously a metaphor for greedy corporations.'

'Pretty sure it's just a kidz book,' a boy called Fungus sed.

'Shut up,' said Mr Dildo. 'Continued Rednoy.'

'The greedy caterpillar can't just eat one apple. He got to go and take a bite of everything, before he becomes a raging butterfly. Likewise, corporations have to keep sucking the life out of society. Rememba wot a tol u, next time you see a bright butterfly flapping about. It may look pretty on the outside, but deep down it's a selfish little creature.'

'How would you sum the book up as a whole?' Mr Dildo asked.

'Overall I'd give it 4 out 5. Good metaphors, good symbolism, a strong main character. I'm docking it a point because the storyline was a bit clichéd. However, my favourite part of the whole book was the holes in the pieces of fruit. This is because if you have a willy that is less than 2 inches in circumference you can fit it through the holes and it feels really nice and is also a nice surprise for someone when they turn the page.'

'Wow Rodney,' Mrs Dildo said, whipping a tyre from his eye. 'That is very deep. I must say, you are like a son to me. I am going to tell you a secret you may need in order to save the world from Henry Ford's oven mitts of doom.' Mr Dildo whispered something in Rodney's ear...

Cuming (HA!) to the Odeon...

It's the 4D cinema experience! Watch movies like you have never done before! For the first time, you can actually feel everything going on in the movie!

Darren: 'Man, am I stoked to be seeing Sin City for the first time! And in 4D no doubt!'

*Bruce Willis shoots that guys nuts off.

Darren: 'Argh! Jesus Christ! Why did I think this was a good idea!'

The 4D cinema experience. When a character dies in the film, you die in real life!

Now that Duncan and Rednoy were back in uni, Zara took them to a restaurant to discuss Henry Ford. They chose to eat at Jon the Sods. They got settled and the waiter came around to take their order for food and drinks. He came to Zara last. 'What will you be having madam?'

'Oh, nothing for me thanks,' said Zara.

'You on a diet?' Rodney asked.

'No, I've just decided to give up eating in order to save money. Costs too much, so I'm giving food up.'

The waiter collected all the menus. 'Will that be all?'

'Can you just check that the meat and potato pie is gluten free please?' Duncan asked. 'I can't eat anything with gluten in it. It gives me severe flatulence problems.'

'I shall check for you, sir.'

The waiter walked into the back, whilst Zara and co discussed Henry Ford and plot related issues, which unlike any other author who would sum up the conversation in a few sentences in this paragraph, I am going to completely skip. The waitror went up to the head chef, Jon the Sod. 'Do the meat and potato pies contain gluten?'

Jon the Sod dropped his knife. 'Cum again?'

'One of our customers asked if the pies contain gluten. It gives him gas problems.'

'Glooton? Bloody glooton? Bloody 'ell. Can't even put bloody glooton in owt now. Argh, sod 'im. I'll bek 'im a bloody pie owt a nowt but glooton. You go tell 'im there's no glooton in us pies and we'll see 'ow much gas 'e's got. Nowt bloody wrong with it. I don't know. Bloody glooton. Whatever next?' Jon the Sod flicked a bogie in the pie for good measure.

'The coke tap is empty,' said the waiter. 'Do you want me to get Max to refill it?'

'Don't be bloody daft. There's some cola ice pops int fridge. Get juice out'ut bottom of them. Don't go wasting money refilling't taps.'

'Will do. Oh, and the lady on table 3 has asked if we have any pasta instead of chips?'

'Give 'em bloody chips. We ant got any o' that foreign muck 'ere.'

30 minutes later Rodney and Duncan received their food. Ten (talk about being inconsistent between choosing to write the word for a number or the actual number) minutes later, Duncan felt like he was going to shit himself. He got the waiters attention. 'Excuse me. I thought you said this didn't contain gluten. Clearly it does, because I feel like I'm about to crap my arse off.'

'Sorry sir, but we have a no complaints policy. Look.' The waiter pointed to a plaque on the wall. It said 'No complaints. Or else.'

'This simply will not!' Ducan shouted. 'I specifically made you aware of my gluten problem and you ignored me. I would like to speak to the manager.'

The waiter went into the back. 'The gluten man wants to speak to you.'

'Oh-aye?' said Jon the Sod.

'He reckons your pie's made him shit himself.'

Jon the Sod groaned. 'I'll bloody make him shit 'imself.' He blew his nose and swapped the tissue with a napkin on a plate about to be served. He swayed out of the kitchen and the waiter pointed him to the table. He swayed over to Duncan and co. 'Did 'e not show y'ut plaque?'

'Mr, I have to say that I am appalled with your service. I have been given gluten after making it clear that I cannot have it. My bowels feel like they're gonna explode.'

Jon the Sod groaned. 'Argh, don't be such a bloody woman. There's nowt bloody wrong with ya. Bit a glooton 'ull do ya good.'

'I must admit,' said Rodney, whilst Duncan trumped. 'My Yorkshire puddings a bit burnt. In fact, the entire things black.'

'Argh, there's nowt bloody wrong with it. Just a bit crispy, that's all. If yer gonna complain, you can make it yer bloody self next time. Now get it darn ya.'

Rodney and Duncan reluctantly ate their food after Jon the Sod'''s lecture. Duncan, unfortunately, died of a dislocated arse. The police came around to investigate and Jon the Sod said, 'There's nowt bloody wrong with 'im. Get a pint o' John Smith's darn 'im, that'll bring 'im too.' The police apologised for wasting Jon the sods time.

Meanwhile, on YouTube...

Green Day – American Idiot (55 million + views)

Comments

Edge_maestro:

This is real music, not like Justin Boobar and One Diversion

RavenThorns:

This generation will never understand real music.

Arma88edon:

@RavenThorns I blame da charts 4 brainwashing da unwashed masses. I guess you cud sayz its 'the meediya kentrolling da nashun'.

English Genius:

Why are you using an @ sign to reply to a comment on youtube, you arsehole?

King_of_punk_rock:

Ur ryt Arma88edon. Green Day is keeping punk rock alive.

Eric 'luvs to strum' Brady:

Punk rock? PUNK ROCK? This is post punk revival. Get it right, sheeple!

Johnny Rotten is GOAT:

LMAO, this isn't punk at all, this is pop music for little fag boys. Real punk fans listen to sex pistols and the clash.

Delluded Barbara:

I dnt care wot music dis is. Sum1 needs 2 ban dis heavy metal crap. Sick of emo music like Food Fighters and Skrillex.

Ruiner of fun:

Guys, cant we just all accept we like different genres of music?

Johnny Rotten is GOAT:

Who invited fag boy to the party?

Molish Mark:

Wow. I cun't believe the 1st man to step on the moon is the lead singer of Green Day.

Sixteen

Phoenix arrived at his parents' home in the middle of a suburban paradise. He was greeted by his mum, Daisy. 'Hia, Milo. I didn't know you were coming to visit us! What a lovely surprise.'

Phoenix pulled a face. 'God, Mum! I told you my name's Phoenix!'

'My, my, you are as adorable as ever, Milo. It's lovely to see you.'

'Calm down, Mum! I'm only here 'cause the stupid government made our dorms unavailable because of fear of terrorist attacks. Now I have to come live here. It's so unfair.'

'Well, it's lovely to see you again.'

'Yeah, yeah, yeah. What's for dinner?'

'I'm sorry, Milo. I've just cooked me and your father dinner.'

'Great! Now I'm gonna starve to death! Thanks a lot, Mum.'

'I'm sorry, honey. I'll cook you something if you are hungry. What would you like?'

'Pizza.'

Daisy looked in the freezer. 'I'm sorry, honey. We don't have any pizza left.'

'Can't Dad go out and get some?' His dad, Jay, entered the kitchen. 'Dad, I need you to get me some pizza.'

'Hey, old sport!' Jay said excitedly. 'I didn't know you were coming home.'

'Dad, seriously. You need to stop calling me old sport. It's totally uncool.'

'My, my, busta. You've grown since we last saw you! Hasn't he grown, dear?'

'My Milo's becoming a big boy fast!'

Phoenix grimaced. 'Erm no, I haven't grown. Don't you know you stop growing at the age of nineteen? Everybody knows that. I probably look taller because you're both old and have crappy memories.'

'Don't talk to me and your mother like that, son.'

'Whatever, bro. Listen, Jay. I need you to go get me a pizza.'

'Please don't call me Jay. I'm your dad.'

'Dad's lame. I prefer Jay. So anyway, about that pizza—'

'All the shops nearby will be shut now, son. But we'll give you some money, so you can order a pizza from the takeaway.'

'Oh for God's sake! So now I have to practically buy my own ingredients and make my own food after a full day at university! Gee, thanks a lot, Dad!' Phoenix stormed out of the room. He came back in seconds later. 'Can I have the money, then?' Jay gave his son the money. Phoenix went upstairs to his bedroom and nervously ordered a takeaway. He switched on the tele, and up came a news report on how Italy had been destroyed. How convenient that was the first thing to come up on the television seen as though it affects the plot...

'BREAKING NEWS! BREAKING NEWS! EVERYBODY PANIC 'CAUSE THERE'S BREAKING NEWS! LET SHIT HIT THE FAN AND THE APOCALYPSE HAPPEN BECAUSE THERE IS BREAKING NEWS!'

The Unlabelled King spoke on the live broadcast. He no longer wore his head sock; there was no point since everyone knew he had a floppy willy on his head. '...this is the despicable action of cowards. No doubt the attack was orchestrated by the Italian mafia or the Catholic church. Because we all know, the only two types of people who can commit acts of terrorism are gangsters and religious people. Fear not, for I am here to restore peace.'

Meanwhile, here's some shameless advertising:

Naked Embarrassments

Do you have a defect so freakishly strange it makes you uncomfortable to go out in public? Does a blemish on your skin cause you great discomfort? Then why not cure your embarrassment, by broadcasting your naked body to the entire nation?

From the man with a tube of Colgate for a nob to the woman with Darth Maul living up her hoot, these people have never been so proud to wear their red faces on television!

Naked Embarrassments: the show that exists because for some fucking reason, people would rather self-degrade themselves on national television than book a private doctor's appointment.

Seventeen

Oldham was a strange town; oddly enough, it was the only town in England solely populated by hippos.

'Yay! We're off to spend the weekend in Oldham!' said nobody, ever. The confirmation they had arrived came from a billboard that said, 'Welcome to Oldham…at least it's not Rochdale.'

Phoenix rocked up with a hulking Italian by his side. Tara looked at Johnny and Rodney to make sure what she saw was real. They shared her confusion. They didn't have to ask. The look on their faces was enough of a question for Phoenix to have to explain himself. 'I'm helping the Italian refugees.'

'Okay,' Tara said. She noticed the Italian looking her over. 'Where are the rest of them?'

'The rest did not survive. He is the only one. His name is Gianluca Speroni.'

Speroni pointed a finger at Phoenix. 'That's General to you.'

'*General* Gianluca Speroni. Here. He's all yours.' Speroni moved within a finger's distance of Tara as soon as Phoenix let him go.

'Hang on a minute,' Tara quickly said before Phoenix could walk off. 'You can't just offload him on us. I thought you said you were helping the refugees?'

'Oh, don't worry,' Phoenix assured her. 'I'm changing all my Instagram posts to pictures of lasagne; that way I will be doing my bit.' Phoenix walked off.

Speroni opened his mouth before Tara could tell him to back off. '*Mamacita!* Forgive me for my half-Italian half-Mexican heritage, but I am trying to swoon you. I would offer you a rose, but all I have in my pocket is a pile of ragù.' Speroni reached inside his pocket and pulled out a pile of ragù.

Tara narrowed her eyes. 'You keep ragù in your pocket?'

'*Si, si.* A little-known stereotype about us Italians is that we are all excessive hoarders. We carry around all kinds of crap in our pockets. See here. Milk in my trouser pocket, in case I get thirsty.' Speroni showed the dripping insides of his pocket. 'And in my coat sleeve, I keep a tub of motor oil, so my hair can permanently look like it has just been dunked in a can of petrol. How is my swooning of you working? Are you ready to sit on my face yet?'

Tara pulled out a Bunsen burner and put it beside Speroni's head, and the grease in his hair was enough to attract the flame that set him ablaze. It took him 180 seconds to find a puddle deep enough to submerge the flames. He emerged with a charred ~~black~~ African American face, but everything was okay because he was related to Wile E. Coyote, and his face went back to normal when the next scene started.

There was no way Speroni hadn't picked up the clues that Tara was uninterested in him. He most definitely had picked up the hints; he just chose to ignore them. They reached the bottom of the well. Speroni stayed at the back—the farthest away from Tara—as they headed down the dark tunnels. He giggled as he tapped Rodney on the shoulder.

'Wot?'

'Here.' Speroni giggled like a schoolgirl as he held out a piece of paper. Rodney's temperature rose as he felt himself becoming a part of a childish carry-on. 'Give this to Tara, please.'

Rodney shook his head. Johnny perked up. 'What does it say?' he asked excitedly. 'What does it say?'

Rodney tapped Tara on the shoulder, ignoring Johnny who was wagging like a dog. She turned around, and he said, 'From the Italian bloke.' She read the piece of paper, screwed it up, and threw it at Speroni's face. She carried on walking.

Johnny bounced up and down. 'What did it say? What did it say?'

'Here.' Speroni handed Johnny the paper. Johnny read it:

'I want to put my leaning tower of Pisa inside your colosseum and thrust back and forth, if ya know what I mean ;)'

Johnny slapped his forehead with his palm. 'Dude. You can't just outright say you want to have sex with her.'

'Why not? That's how it works in Italy.'

'But you're in Britain now, and in Britain, women love a gentleman.'

'Gentle man? I am confused by your use of these two words as one.'

'A gentleman. A chivalrous, courteous, or honourable man.'

Johnny would later go on to be arrested for plagiarism after that comment. 'A gentleman performs acts of kindness for his woman.'

'*Qué?* But I thought placing myself inside her was a kind act.'

'Dude, you need to start off a bit more delicate—like buying her a bouquet of flowers.'

'Oh, I see. Like inviting the old man off the Dolmio advert around, so he can shout "When'sa your Dolmio Day?" in her face?'

'Err, maybe not. Here, I'll help.'

Most humans can shut their eyes. After listening to some of the painful ideas Johnny and Speroni shared with each other, Rodney wished he could shut his ears. In the end, Speroni and Johnny came up with:

'*My lady Tara. Ta-ra. A sweet two-trickle step off the teeth. Ta, for the sound of your beautiful voice when you are saying thank you for something. Ra, for when you are doing an impression of a dinosaur. You are the prettiest of all petals, and I would be ever so humbled to hold your hand and be your protector. I, your protector, will be there when the builders are catcalling you. I will stride up to them and say, "Hey, you fat, smelly builder. How dare you treat her like an object. Only I may overbear her with my clinginess." I would leave them so embarrassed that they would apologise to you, and then I would kiss the hand of may fair lady. I'd kiss you in Leicester Square, Whitechapel Road, and even in jail. I will ring you up hourly to make sure you are okay, and I will give you foot massages and pamper you with cuddles and kisses for at least nineteen of the twenty-four hours in each day. I am sure you would not find my obsession with you nauseating or off-putting at all. I can be the man of your dreams.*'

Satisfied, they handed the note to Rodney. Rodney sighed as he prodded Tara on the back again. 'From them.'

She looked back at the excited duo. She read one word of the note before writing something on the back of it. She threw it back at Speroni. Giddily, he and Johnny read what she had put:

'*I will never have sex with you. Ever.*'

Speroni laughed. 'Playing hard to get, are we?'

'I don't know,' Johnny said. 'That message sounds pretty clear.'

The message would never be clear to Speroni. 'Nonsense. There is still a chance. I have not even pulled out my final trick yet.'

Speroni reached inside one of his many pockets and pulled out a walkie-talkie. He yelled and soon the ### soon arrived in the well.

'What's the problem?' the ### asked in a mysterious voice.

'It's Tara,' Speroni said, dead seriously. 'I can't get through to her. I need you to chat her up for me.'

'I'm on it.' The ### zoomed down the tunnel to Tara, which was incredibly unnecessary considering she was only a few yards away from Speroni.

Tara looked the figure over. 'Who the hell are you?'

'I'm the fastest man alive.'

'Lightning McQueen?'

'Lightning McQueen's a car, you moron.'

'Wait a minute. You're the ###. You're ###, aren't you? What do you want?'

'I am coming to the aid of my amigo. Speroni is a good man with a kind heart. You just have to give him a chance.'

'Oh for goodness' sake. Why are you doing this? Has anyone throughout the history of time ever gotten a girlfriend by getting their mate to win an argument with the girl they're pursuing over whether they should go out with them or not?'

'Fair dos. Will you go out with me instead?'

'No.'

'Come on. We can do everything really quick. We can have dinner and go to the movies in super-fast time.'

'You can watch movies in super-fast time?'

'Of course. It takes me nine seconds to watch the entire Lord of the Rings trilogy.'

'That doesn't sound very enjoyable.'

'Nonsense. It just leaves more room for making love, nyha-ha-ha-ha.'

'By the sounds of how quick you do everything, that doesn't sound very good either.' And with that cutting insult, the ### burst into tears. He ran to the edge of the Grand Canyon and slowed down as he stepped over the edge.

After a long stroll, they finally came to the fiery core that lay beneath Oldham. All, except Rodney who couldn't care less, put their hands over their mouths in shock. They watched the Unlabelled

King's past blaze inside a sunlit diamond. The King planned to make the world more efficient by using jealousy as a form of currency, but when the UN laughed at his idea, he vowed revenge on the world. One frightful day, he found a magic pen that granted him any wish he wanted. He wished to make himself the god of his own world, and he rewrote the commandments on what it took to live a life of good moral:

Thou shalt do thy utmost best to set trends, then shun everyone when they actually follow them

Thou shalt only ever order the most obscure meal on every restaurant menu

Thou shalt pretend to have read and understood Finnegans Wake

Thou shalt go on a gap year to Africa and take big smiley pictures of thyself with the malnourished African children

Thou shalt secretly condemn the children when thou cometh back with malaria

He was the King who ruled on vengeance. What weakness did he have?

'Of course,' Johnny said as the image inside the diamond turned to one of the King on his throne. 'The wall behind him.' A giant crack ran down the middle of the wall.

'Look,' Tara said, pointing at a green ring of light on the ground. Inside the ring was a hammer. She looked at the weapon, then at the wall. The hammer came with an obligatory tutorial that 'wielding the weapon isn't a case of heavy strikes but is more like a dance,' which you'll all be happy I'm going to skip out. Anyhow, Tara knew what needed to be done.

Progress Review Dos: The same as the first, but worse due to lack of novelty.

'Ah, Mr Travis. Welcome back to Secondary School.'

I don't get w—

'Hush! Put your hand up if you wish to speak.'

…

…

I've got my bloody hand up.

'Language, young man! Or would you like me to send you to the headmaster's office? Wait silently, until I decide to stop pretending that I haven't seen your hand even though it has been flailing about in the air clear for everyone to see. What you gonna do about it? You gonna put your hand down? Nah, because you need my attention. You'll hold it up till it wants to fall out of its socket, bitch. In the meantime, sit down on that stool, which for whatever reason has a hole in the centre of it.'

In my experience, Miss, I think that hole is there so someone can shove their ruler up the other side.

'I don't know. I reckon it's there just in case you're desperate for a poo during the middle of lesson. Ah, school. I bet you're glad to be back. They say the best days of your life are at school.'

Pardon me, Miss, but I reckon whoever made that quote up must have gone on a downward spiral in later life.

'What do you dislike about school, Rimjob Travis? Oops, excuse me for calling you by your middle name. Let us wait for the rest of the class to stop heckling you for your hilarious middle name. Now then, rimmy Bill, what do you hate about school?'

Everything. If I had to do it all over again, I wouldn't bother going. I can just picture it now: "Hello Billy, I am your new science teacher. Today you are going to be boiling water using a Bunsen burner. Oh, you think that's boring? Don't worry; we'll sit you next to the local school arsonist. That way you'll be on your toes for the next year. Meanwhile, because I am such a good teacher, I will turn a blind eye every time he tries to set your face on fire." No. You won't see me in a school again.

'Oh, don't be so melodramatic. School is designed to get you used to life in the real world.'

I'm pretty sure I've never seen anybody in public fire pieces of their cut-up rubber at anyone.

'Yet for all your complaints, you are back here, because obviously your brain has deteriorated since you left. You will now get your writing help from the high school. That's right, the same place that thought it would be a good idea to teach Shakespeare to a bunch of teenagers more concerned about who could slap the other person's hands the quickest. Whoever put together the English curriculum is a genius. Yes, I can just see us all watching a video of *A Midsummer Night's Dream* that looked like it was filmed in the twelfth century. Motherfucking genius. If *Much Ado About Nothing* was written today, it would be called *A Lot of Fuss About Fuck All*.'

If *Much Ado About Nothing* was written today, it would be critically deemed good for about three months, before someone on the Internet would say it's overrated, then everybody would change their tune and say they didn't like it.

'I'll give you that one, Billy. That is the rule of life. Everything shit is shit, and everything good is eventually shit anyway.'

You're gonna have me take inspiration from Shakespeare, then?

'Hand, you little shit.'

…

…

…

'And that's my first rule of writing. You put in ellipsis to express that you had put your hand up and were waiting for me to answer you, when the reader is obviously too stupid to see what you were doing.'

Ellipsis? What you chatting? I've been sat here with my hand up.

'Smart arse. Back to my original point—you are describing the actions all wrong. You must have never been on Tumblr. This is what all the cools kids are doing now. Watch and read.'

*Miss holds up hand.

'See. That is how you write actions that people can clearly understand.'

Wow!

*pulls out cock and has a wank.

That's fantastic, Miss. Got any more tips?

'Always, without fail, finish every single chapter on a cliffhanger. Screw that, finish every single paragraph on a cliffhanger.'

That sounds a little formulaic, predictable and slightly tedious.

'Why do you say that?'

Because spontaneity is all we really have, isn't it? As soon as you realise you're reading a story you've already read, the excitement disappears. Lots of books follow similar patterns, and filling my work with cliffhangers isn't going to help it be unique.

'Do you wanna be unique, or do you wanna make money? Of course you want to make money, you greedy little brat. After all, that's the end goal of school. To make ~~us~~ you pig rich.'

True dat. Any more advice?

'Adverbs, Billy. Use an adverb to describe every bit of dialogue any character says. A top tip is to add *y* onto the end of any word. Also, make sure to throw in a few questions throughout your story to insult the reader's intelligence.'

Wow!

*blows Miss a kiss.

Thanks, Miss. I am sure to write the greatest story of all time now.

Eighteen

Rodney had no choice but to carry the hammer back to Bradford. Tara was too busy distancing herself from Speroni, while Johnny had suddenly diagnosed himself with vaginitis.

'You mean arthritis?' Rodney asked questioningly.

'Whatever, dude,' Johnny replied nonchalantly.

Rodney carried the hammer in a carrier bag. It was branded a 'bag for life,' which would have been accurate had the holder been born in the middle of no-man's land. They arrived back in Bradford. Johnny gasped. A crowd was gathered around the jobcentre; amid them stood...The Unlabelled King.

'You go on,' Tara suggested bravely to the rest. 'I will distract the King. Use the hammer to destroy his wall while he is not there,' she expounded lazily.

Rodney, Speroni, and Johnny continued toward the abstract art museum. Suddenly, a vortex ripped through the atmosphere. Out popped a mysterious man...Ed Boner.

'Ed Boner?' Johnny questioned askingly.

'Yes. It is I. Ed Boner,' Ed Boner proclaimed valiantly. 'I am afraid I can't let you do what you are about to do. Now you will see my true form,' he laughed hysterically. Suddenly, a ginormous bulge burst out of his zipper. The trio gasped when they realised what it was. It was Ed Boner's erect penis.

'Now you see my twenty-inch shlong—fear me!' Ed shouted loudly. The trio ducked and dived as Ed tried to crush them with his colossal wanga.

'Somebody help us!' Johnny shouted frightenedly. Suddenly, Rodney received the power of superhuman strength. However, he didn't know how to turn it on, so he couldn't use it.

'Fear not,' Speroni said Italianly. 'I have faced things like this before.'

WEE WOO WEE WOO!

Suddenly, sirens went off. But nobody had reported a crime. Why, then, did a police car pull in beside them?

'Who are you?' Rodney asked jadedly.

'We are the preposition police. We are here to arrest that greasy man for ending a sentence with a preposition,' the policeman explained speakingly.

'Oh. You're one of them pedantic arseholes?' Rodney questioned dryly.

'Pedantic? We're just following the laws of language, man,' the policeman said clearly. 'This Italian must add words to that sentence, or else he's going to jail.'

'You can't be serious?' Rodney asked angrily. 'You know what he meant. You're going to crucify him for something that clear?'

The policeman slapped cuffs around Speroni's wrists. 'He will finish his sentence. Won't you Italian?' the policeman asked demandingly.

Speroni said awkwardly, 'I was going to say that I have faced things like this before going to the dog masseuse.'

'That's much better. We'll let you go now,' the policeman said kindly, yet not unkindly. Suddenly, Ed's boner crashed down and killed one of the policemen. He shot daggers from his eyes at the shaking onlookers of the public. LITERAL daggers that pierced them all. This just in: eight members of the public dead.

A long-lost emotion rose in Rodney's core. It was a pang of fear. It was a pang of feeling. It was a reminder that inside his heartless body he was still alive, and by God was he ready for his life to end. That was why he was overcome with anxiety. Ed's penis could crush him any second, and he would have to go to the gruelling afterlife God had created, robbing him of the eternal rest he desperately craved. Suddenly, a gorilla fell from the sky.

Speroni wonderingly said, 'Maybe we can kill the thing from the inside.'

WEE WOO WEE WOO!

'That's it, Mr Italian! You're going to jail!' the preposition police chief shouted not quietly, as they handcuffed Speroni and took him away. Suddenly, a gun appeared in Rodney's hand for whatever reason.

He lined up the shot to save his soul from damnation. He had never used a gun before. He could not keep his trembling hands still. 'Don't worry,' Johnny said soothingly. 'Imagine it's a massive cock.'

All of a sudden, Rodney fell over a gorilla lying in the middle of the road.

Ed's boner loomed over Rodney. Lying on his back, he kicked the gun toward Johnny. 'Quick!' Rodney shouted hastily. 'Pop a cap in his ass!' Johnny put down the gun, took off his hat, and tried to shove it between Ed's butt cheeks. 'What the hell are you doing?' Rodney shouted tensely.

'You told me to put a cap in his arse. I'm only doing what you said,' Johnny said saidingly. Out of nowhere, Ed caught him with a back kick. Johnny rubbed his red face and said angrily, 'That's it, boner boy. You're going down.'

WEE WOO WEE WOO!

'That's a violation of the law!' the preposition police chief shouted loudly.

'You've got to be kidding,' Rodney said, not jokingly. 'What he just said is so understandable, it isn't even funny. You can't possibly be that finicky.'

'In case you didn't know, we're the preposition police,' the police chief said clearly. 'We're part of the literacy emergency services. Of course we would be that fussy to throw a paddy over a sentence that ends with a preposition. The fact is, your friend didn't state down where be Ed's location. Therefore, we must arrest him.'

Johnny said awkwardly, 'Um…I meant he was going down the toilet?'

'Too late for that, pal,' the police chief said clearly. The showdown became only two: Rodney and Ed Boner. Suddenly, Rodney tripped over a gorilla lying in the middle of the road.

Ed Boner licked his lips as his mammoth todger shadowed over Rodney. Evilly, he said, 'Now that I have you right where I want you, let me spew dialogue for absolutely no reason whatsoever before I even try to make an attempt to kill you. I could end you quickly and in seconds and accomplish all that I have set out to do, but instead, I shall waffle on some more. Then, and only after I have stalled for however long is humanly possible, will I deal the blow that ends you. RAH-HA-HA!' Rodney was in a deadly predicament. Surely he was going to die? Ed swung his penis down, when suddenly…

'BAH GAWD, KING! IT'S THE GORILLA!'

The gorilla that had tripped up Rodney got to its feet. Ed Boner shat his pants as he watched the beast march toward him. Suddenly, Rodney pulled Ed down by the tights and rolled him up.
1!
2!
3!
Ding, ding, ding!

'BAH GAWD, KING! RODNEY HAS DONE IT! HE'S BECOME WORLD CHAMPION! BY GAWD, DEUS EX MACHINA IS RUNNING WILD!'

Then the Gorilla threw a grenade on the ground and blew everyone up. Was Rodney dead?

Nineteen

No, he wasn't. He's back in the next chapter. Anyway…

Tara marched straight through the crowd. 'You!' The crowd turned to her as she pointed at the Unlabelled King. She could feel the showdown coming. She was the whaler, and her enemy was Moby Dick—or in this case, Moby Dickhead.

'You again. What is the meaning of this? I thought I warned you,' the Unlabelled King said, scowling. He suddenly smiled. 'On second thoughts, go on. Try to do me with your little shenanigans. That Internet stunt only increased my power, never mind Italy.'

'There you have it, people!' Tara shouted at the crowd. 'He doesn't care about any of you. He doesn't want a better world. He just wants more popularity.'

'Nonsense. I am a man of the people. Why do you think I am at the jobcentre? Because I can relate to the unemployed. Just because I am the King doesn't mean I'm not entitled to claim jobseeker's allowance. After all, I do about as much work as everybody else here. Right, everybody?'

And everybody cheered, 'Yeah!'

Tara shook her head. 'You people can't be brainwashed this easily, can you?'

'Of course they can,' the Unlabelled King bellowed. 'As proof, here's this morning's newspaper.'

This just in: David Cameron cures AIDS and saves baby from burning building while doing it.

The crowd cheered, 'God bless David Cameron! He is a national treasure.'

'Now,' the Unlabelled King said. 'Let's have a look at tomorrow's newspaper.'

Breaking news: David Cameron spotted taking a dump in homeless man's coin collection.

The crowd booed. 'That rotten David Cameron! I always knew he was a nasty piece of work!'

Tara's jaw dropped. 'You can't all be this easily swayed?'

'You're just bitter,' the Unlabelled King shouted. 'I'll have you all know this woman didn't shed a tear for this year's X-factor winner's sob story.' The entire crowd gasped. 'That's right! Get her!'

The public hunted Tara with no remorse. The angry mob closed in on Tara, and for the second chapter in a row, a holy spirit came to save the hero. What are the chances of that?

This time, it was God's turn to help Tara for the faith she had put in him. He soared from the sky, crashing ball bag first over the masses. He stretched his sack out like a puddle and suffocated everyone. Tara celebrated. 'Gee whizz! Thanks, God!'

'No worries, fam. Now I have save world, I go.'

'Hang on, God. The King is still there. God? God?' For whatever reason, God had not killed the biggest threat. Instead, he did what was stereotypical of him and ignored Tara. Tara watched him ascend back to Heaven. She turned back to the Unlabelled King. She cracked her fingers. 'Looks like it's just me and you.'

'Listen, before y—hang on, you were supposed to die two chapters ago.'

'What? Oh…Hang on. God said pretty early on he couldn't get involved, but he just did.'

'All the more reason for people to hate him and love me! Now anyway, you should be dead.'

'No, you.'

'Nope.' Then a boiler plummeted down from the sky and crushed Tara. Ha! I bet you thought that was a typo back in chapter three, didn't you? Now who looks stupid! You shouldn't be such a smartarse now, should you?

?

It was 1-1 during the New York City, New York Red Bulls derby and both teams had already used all 3 subs with 20 minutes still to go. Joe London was already on a yellow card. He knew the next time the ball came to him he was going to pick it up so he could get his second yellow. He had to. He was absolutely dying for a shit.

How now he regretted campaigning against FIFA God Sepp Blatter. He thought back to the man's time in power. 'Introducing de new brown card,' Sepp Blatter had announced. 'Now when footballer needs to go poo, the referee will give him de brown card.' FIFA God was laughed out of the room at the time, but now Joe saw the genius idea for what it was.

The ball wasn't coming anywhere near him. *That's it*, Joe thought in italics. *Time to take action into my own hands.* He was just going to have to foul someone—right now. *Ready?* 'Uriah Rennie.'

He walked over to the opposizshuns goalkeeper and gave him a swirly. The referee charged over. *This is it*, Joe thought with a grin. But before the referee could pull out his card he stopped.

A pang of shock hit Joe. 'What are you baby booing?' he said. 'Send us whooping cough.' But the referee heard not a word he said. Nor did anybody else. New York's eyes were fixed on a menacing duck egg blue cloud that loomed in the sky.

Suddenly, duck egg blue laser beams fired down on everyone. The crowd screamed and ran as they tried to avoid the onslaught. The players headed for the tunnel. *Thank God the world's ending, Joe thought. At least I can sneak off and have a shit before it does. Fuck that. I don't need to sneak off. The world's ending. I'll have a shit here. Also, why am I thinking in coherent sentences? Do people actually think in paragraphs of text in real life? I don't think this is an accurate portrayal of thoughts.*

Joe pulled his shorts down and heaved. It didn't bother him that the last thing he would see was Frank Lampard's appalled eyes staring at him. He was proud to stain the Yankee Stadium. Suddenly, the lasers stopped shooting. Turned out the end of the world wasn't so abrupt. 'You're having a tin bath,' Joe moaned. The crowd came back. The players came back. Everybody looked at him with his pants down and the turd between his legs. The referee pulled out the straight red. Joe was sent off.

Meanwhile, Zaza and Rednoy arrived in New York. They watched the Hudson River fill up with oil. 'Come on,' said Rodney. 'We have to save Earth.'

?

Rodney and Zara sailed for New York after Mrs Dildo had told Rodney that that was where the final battle to save the world would commence—because we all know, battles to save the world are only allowed to take place in New York.

Rodney couldn't settle. His ex-girlfriend lived under the sea and he didn't want to bump into her. Just then, a Walrus came by, floating on a giant piece of bread. 'Hello,' said Mr Walrus. 'Do you have any de-icer? I am trying to melt the polar icecaps so I can move my car.'

'Sorry,' said Rodney. 'I do not have any de-icer. I will try to leave all of my house lights on during the middle of the day if that helps?'

'Nice one bud. Also, in a comment that has nothing to do with what we're talking about, Int It's a shame what happened to Ford Henry.'

'Wait?' said Zara. 'What happened to him?'

'He went and got his face blown off didn't he? Anyhow, I'm off on vacation to Jamaica for a week. I might even get a tan.'

Rednoy and Zaza continued to sail towards New York. They looked at giant duck egg blue clouds looming over the city. 'If Thierry Henry's ford is dead,' Rednoy asked. 'Who's responsible for that?'

Chapter Comblax

Rednoy and Zaza entered the duck egg blue bubble submerging New York.

'Fools!' shouted the man in duck egg blue as he floated down from the ground. It couldn't be? I COULDN'T BEE! OH NO!

Zara and Rednoy gasped. 'No,' they gasped. 'It can't be,' they gasped. 'ITZ THE MAN IN DUCK EGG BLUE!!!!!!'

'That's right you cunt heads! I am finally back ffrom planet Comblex! I am control oil! I even made the most powerful substance known to man, comblax 9, and all I got was a back rub! I've had it! It's my time to show the world what I can do!'

The man in duck egg blue fired all of the comblax 9 in the world into the air. Suddenly, the birds began to shit nuclear bombs. The world leaders, the good ones and the dickhead ones, all came together to try to stop the disaster but ended up cumming in each other's hair. Everybody was dead, except for Mugabe who was in space.

Take note Marvel. I have given you the villain for your next blockbuster film. Do it!

Da End

Twenty

*Johnny scratches head.

'That was odd. We won in the end. But how? Oh well. Any victory is a victory.'

'We did *buona*, my English *amico*. *Noi* are *eroi*.'

'Why has your English suddenly turned terrible?'

'Because as well as missing out words, that is easiest way to portray foreigner, my friend. Now I must leave. It has been pleasure fighting with you.'

*Speroni holds out hand. Johnny shakes it.

'But where will you go now, General Speroni?'

'Don't worry about me. Your Prime Minister has already offered us Italians refuge in the north of Great Britain, in return for getting rid of the Scottish.'

'Good luck to you, and remember to tag me in a Facebook status in two years' time stating that you have missed me, even though you've made no effort to get in contact with me during that time. Good-bye, my friend. Rodney, aren't you going to say good-bye to Speroni? Rodney?'

*Rodney raises arms to the sky.

'Okay, God. I did everything you wanted me to do. I'm waiting.'

*A vortex ripples through the sky. God pops out of the other end of an arsehole. A big trump noise is made as vortex closes.

'I'm here, baby boy. What do you want?'

'You promised me that if I got rid of the Unlabelled King, you'd let me die.'

'But don't you see, Rodney? This hasn't just been a quest. This has been a spiritual journey for you to find your soul and a new lease of life. You have played with new friends, seen new sights, and witnessed what a hard life really is so that you may appreciate your own life. What do you say, pal? Wanna give life another go?'

'No. Kill me.'

'All right. Suit yourself.'

*God wrecks Rodney.

The End

Twenty-One

Rodney arrived at the entrance of the abstract art lair, when Speroni and Johnny pulled in beside him. Any peace he had from being alone died. He frowned. 'Why are you two here? I thought you were in jail.'

'Ha-ha, the General has his ways!' Speroni laughed. 'On the way to preposition prison, I asked the officers if I could stop off and buy a lottery ticket.'

'Let me guess. You did a runner when they weren't looking?'

'Nope. I purchased the lottery ticket. And you'll never guess what…I had the winning numbers! They let us out our cells, so we could collect our winnings. Just like when you win the jackpot card in monopoly.'

'What the hell are you talking abo—'

'Who'd have thought picking one to seven would have won me eighty billion pounds?'

'I call bullshit. There's no way you won that amount of money.'

'It was an eight-year rollover.'

'Even so. With the numbers one to seven?'

'Why not? You have just as much chance with any other seven numbers.'

'That's just…Okay, I'll give you that one.'

Johnny looked up at the stars as if he were dreaming. 'I wish I won the lottery,' he said. 'I'd resign and go on the dole.'

'Here's what's wrong with that,' Rodney said. 'One. We just had a joke about a rich guy being on the dole in the last chapter. Two. You wouldn't need to go on the dole, 'cause you'd be rich.'

'I know I wouldn't need to go on the dole. I'd do it for the banter.'

Rodney had not the energy to respond to that. He ignored them as they went through the museum and entered the King's room. All he had to do was hit the back wall with the hammer. Suddenly, the King popped up from behind the throne. 'Not so fast!'

'King Dickhead? But how did you get here?' Johnny questioned.

'I told you a long time ago how my smug powers work. My powers are at an all-time high, especially after God appeared for the first time since BC and killed a few people—even when he tries to do good, he makes himself look like an idiot. I used the power I absorbed to fly back here and ruin your little crusade. Now I will destroy you, just like I destroyed Tara.'

'I'm sick of your crap,' said Rodney. 'You say you run on smugness, but we all know that's just a gimmick. You have a secret behind that wall we know for a fact you're hiding from the world. You're so insecure that you've given yourself a persona that enables you to look down upon everyone. You claim to be open-minded and sophisticated, but people who are open-minded and sophisticated don't hate everything. I may be a miserable bastard, but at least I admit it. You're a miserable bastard who pretends to be enlightened. I can't wait to kill you, so I can rest in peace.'

The King's veins tightened in his moustache. 'Watch your tongue. Do you forget who you are talking to? Do you forget my power? I will annihilate you. I'll eviscerate you without giving you the chance to rest in peace. I'll pull every last one of your puny organs out of your body, and just before your last breath, I'll strap you to a life-support machine. You'll weep at my feet when I humble you.'

'That's where you're wrong, King. You can break every bone in my body. You can send me home in an ambulance, and you can rip my face off with a chainsaw, but I'll never be humbled by you, 'cause you're a dickhead.' Rodney pulled the hammer out of the bag for life and hurled it at the back wall. Hey! Wait! No!

Bang!

Oh, bollocks.

'Hey. You're that guy who's not shut up since that night I jumped off the bridge. I recognise your voice.'

Well done, Rodney. You have solved the real mystery of King Dickhead. I was King Dickhead all along, Rodney. I set you up this entire time. How does it feel to know that I have been writing your destiny the whole time?

'Depends. Are you going to let me rest in peace?'

Nope.

'Then I'm angry, and I'm going to smack this hammer over your head.'

Woah! Swing and a miss! Ha-ha. You might as well just give up,

Fuck sake. The odd numbers are on the wrong side. How's that hap—

Rodney. You can't do anything, because I am writing your destiny. I've written everything you've ever said. I've decided every feeling you've ever had, even the disdain you feel for me right now. You don't have to hate me; I've just written you that way. The only way you can win is if I decide to kill myself. The odds are massively stacked against you. There is no way you are going to defeat me. The author is a carny, Rodney. Whoever loses loses, and whoever wins still loses. The author is a god, Rodney. Just like the massive pair of testicles that look over you, I decide every action everybody makes. I decide who goes to Heaven and Hell before they've even been born. I can do anything to you. See here:

'I am Rodney, and I am going to do a poo in my pants. I just pooed my pants.'

Ha-ha! I told you I could make you do anything. Now, Johnny, you will give yourself a wedgie. Ha-ha! And you, Speroni, you will admit to the whole world you have head lice. Ha-ha! I am going to kick your arse, Rodney. I'll be back, once I have signed off for my parcel…

Thank goodness that guy has gone. Talking out loud was annoying enough, but shouting ha-ha every other second was the last straw. Hang on, why am I talking to myself? Oh well. At least I didn't order a package to Costa Coffee. What weirdo does that? I wonder how long he'll be. Maybe I'll check his laptop. Oh, he's writing a story, is he? Well, this thing reads dreadfully. At least he's written a full novel, near enough. I suppose I could nick his laptop, finish it off myself, and attempt to make some money off it. Or I could just swap the last two chapters over to confuse everyone. Anyone in here object if I steal that weirdo's laptop?

Steal the thing already! I'm sick of nutjobs coming in here and talking to themselves!

Sorry. I'll be off, then.

Comic Con

Hello, everyone, it be me, Billy Travis. I am happy to be here in good old San Diego. Now I will take your questions. First up, Bobby from Sunderland.

Hi, Billy, big fan. Would you like to come around to my house for tea? We can play on Crash Bandicoot?

Sorry, Bob. I prefer to do my homework. Next question, Lyle from Iowa.

Hi, Billy. My question is regarding the original series of HtPaT. In episode 110, Officer Nancy, a British police officer, pulls out a gun to shoot an insect. If you'd have done your research, you'd know British police officers don't use guns. I was enjoying the book up until this moment of unrealism ruined everything for me. Unfortunately for you, I don't miss a trick. I know how everything in the world works. Now tell me, are you just stupid for not knowing how things actually are, or are you lazy?

Well, Lyle…

Also, in episode 119, a giant pair of testicles comes down from the sky and suffocates a crowd of people. This scene was ridiculous. Everybody knows testicles are make-believe. I should know because I've never seen a pair in my life. I would expect this kind of fanatical monster in a fairy tale, not in works that are supposed to mimic real life. I have clearly seen through the false reality you have tried to portray. How does it feel to know you can't fool me?

Mr Lyle…

You know what, this is beyond a joke. I mean, look at us now. Do you even know how Comic Con works? You expect me to suspend my disbelief when there's a guy from Sunderland—which I happen to know is a dump in the north of England because I know everything—at a convention in San Diego? Do you know who you're dealing with? Bitch, I put my mum in a headlock at the age of one when she told me Santa was real. In fact, I refuse to enjoy anything that isn't 100 percent realistic. I will not have my intelligence insulted by anyone anymore. You're not trying to provide easy entertainment, no sir; you're providing us propaganda for how you want people to think the world works. I shan't stand for it anymore. From now on, I shall only watch sports and documentaries. Good day, sir.

???

I'm glad that's done. Now, where the hell am I?

'You know where you are, Billy Travis. You are in the presence of a giant pair of testicles.'

God? Is that you?

'I'm whatever you say I am, Billy. You're writing this dialogue.'

You're right. You know, maybe this proves that something could have created God…

'Sorry, Billy. We already had to suffer through your pretentious religious essay back in chapter six.'

You sure it was chapter six?

'I don't know. You're the one typing this. Just do Ctrl-F.'

Yeah, dint think it wo chapter 6. Chapter 7 m8. Tell us why am ere den?

'Because, Billy Cumstain-Knickers, not only am I God, but I am also a publisher. I have seen the manuscript you have submitted. I'm afraid your story is not like every other story ever, so we cannot publish your work.'

Dagnabbit!

'Language!'

Soz ard. Fuck sake is what I meant to say. Whose arse I gotta kiss to get published, then?

'For a start, you can suck my cheesy left nut. Afterward, rewrite your last chapter so that it has a happy ending. Put in some forced message about positivity, or friendship, or something soppy like that in it.'

Sound.

Chapter Twenty revisited (ft new narrator)

'I'm free!' shouted Rodney. But as he looked back at the happy faces of Speroni and Johnny, he realised he had been free all along. God, who was now a wise old man in a gray cloak—you're damn right that was the letter *a*—came to Rodney from the sky.

'You have a big choice to make, young man,' God said, grinning as he fingered his muzzle. 'Do you love life enough to stay?'

'I have something to say,' Rodney said, with a tear of joy in his eye. 'I've found out the truth. I've found out the truth that in the end, light always conquers evil. Who cares if I'm a loser with a dead-end job and a Rottweiler for a girlfriend? We may not be able to go one minute without insulting one another, but that's what love is, he-ha-hi-ho. Who cares that I'm in my mid-twenties without anything to show for it? As TV has proven, you don't have to do anything. Everything will eventually just sort itself out for the better. I have almost all I need right here.' Rodney put his arms around his friend's shoulders. Speroni shed a single tear. Rodney lowered his head and sighed. 'I just wish Tara was here to see this.'

'Don't count me out yet!'

Rodney lifted his head up at the sound of the sassy shout. 'Tara? TYRAGHHHHHH! B-b-b-but how?'

'I am a main character of this quest. Therefore, I am resistant to death, even if I die.'

Rodney frolicked through the meadow toward his woman. Speroni and Johnny jumped up and down as they roared in celebration. God chortled as he wiped a bead of sweat from his brow. Rodney got down on one knee. 'M'lady. Will you marry…No, wait.' He looked at his friends and beamed a huge grin. 'Will you marry *us*?'

Tara couldn't contain her labia's delight. 'Yes!'

'She said yes!' cried Rodney. 'She said yes!' All was wonderful and gay and merry. The lads took it in turns to suck each other off, while they queued up one by one to stick their fingers inside Tara. And on that day, depression was cured, and nobody miserable ruined anything ever again. THE END

Backword

Self-aggrandizement at its finest. Did-a-chick? You can all suck my dick.
—Stephen King

Letter

Dear Mr Crevis,

I am writing to inform you that Mr Billy Travis is suing you for plagiarism. Further details will be sent to you within the coming weeks. We look forward to seeing you in court.

Letter

Dear Mr Travis,

We are writing to inform you that we at undisclosed greedy
corporation have purchased the rights to use the alphabet. Therefore,
we will be pressing charges against you. We look forward to suing
you for breathing soon.

Printed in Great Britain
by Amazon

53339275R00098